LIFE IS TO LIVE TOGETHER

[LIVE TOGETHER LIKE BUNCH OF FLOWERS OF DIFFERENT COLOURS AND PLEASANT SMELL]

"THE PURPOSE OF LIFE IS TO LIVE IT, TO TASTE EXPERIENCE TO THE UTMOST, TO REACH OUT EAGERLY AND WITHOUT FEAR FOR NEWER AND RICHER EXPERIENCE." - ELEANOR ROOSEVELT

PRAHALAD RAO

BlueRose ONE.com
Stories Matter
NewDelhi • London

BLUEROSE PUBLISHERS
India | U.K.

BlueRose ONE
Stories Matter
NewDelhi • London

For permissions requests or inquiries regarding this publication, please contact:

BLUEROSE PUBLISHERS
www.BlueRoseONE.com
info@bluerosepublishers.com
+91 8882 898 898
+4407342408967

ISBN: 978-93-6261-686-9

Cover design: Tahira
Typesetting: Tanya Raj Upadhyay

First Edition: May 2024

Dedicated to

My wife, Smt. Premila who passed away on 7th December, 2013 due to brain stroke leaving behind her the happiness of living together, more so, in most testing times in life that remember now more than before.

DISCLAIMER

Views expressed by the author in this book are based on his personal understanding of the past and perception of the present. This book neither intends nor suggests any attribution of whatsoever nature to anyone or to any policy or program or system existing or envisaged nor this book intends or suggests to hurt sentiments of any person or state or political bodies or religious bodies or political or religious leaders or body of any other nature or defame any of them whatsoever and any construction of the writings in this book otherwise is sole to the person so construing. The author or the publisher will not be liable for any civil or criminal proceedings under the laws of the country.

GRATITUDES

My gratitude to Dr. Sharda, K.Ananth Raman, Royal Hotel, Hyderabad, late V.Laxma Reddy, late T.S.Murthy, late A.R.Venkataraman, late P.P.S.Puri, late A.S.Dhupia, R.B. Mathur and late Lalit Chand, whose guidance, benevolence and humanism in my initial years of service will shine in my heart for ever, C.V.Nair, late D. Sankaraguruswamy, Dr. Uddesh Kohli, B.M. Pant, M. Prasad, T.N. Thakur, A.A. Khan, Dr. K. K. Govil and Raji Phillips who gave confidence and lent support to me during my most testing time of life.

My gratitude to senior Indian Administrative Officers (IAS) who headed the organizations, account and audit service officers, eminent engineers, eminent finance & legal experts with whom I had the opportunity to work in one capacity or the other during my thirty years of service in public sector Financial Institutions. Gratitudes to late A.K.Sah and Shahzad Bahadur for giving me opportunity to develop my career as a consultant post retirement. My gratitude and special thanks to Dr.J.T.Verghese who offered me chance for continuity of my consultancy job with continued guidance and advice. My association with all of them helped imbibe in me their direction, dedication to the cause of economic development, virtues, values, compassion and affection that became bedrock of my life.

My gratitude to Scholars, Journalists, Thinkers, Philosophers, Historians, Bankers, Economists, Professionals, Socialists and Environmentalists within and outside the country whose writings on Google website helped me to understand the width and depth of subjects selected for this book. Author made an earnest effort to disclose the sources of valuable writings relied upon within the book but due to certain constraints, he was unable to do so, their titles are given under "References" and also stated in the book at some places. The author, wherever considered so necessary, in the public interest, has taken the liberty to reproduce the writings of eminent writers within the ambit of the Copyright Law. Author reiterates his grateful thanks to all of them.

My special thanks to Google for providing inspiration with invaluable sources of information that helped me in completing this book.

In particular, my personal and special gratitude to Arun Kumar Sarna who gave me strong standing support during my association with him in service in multi-national consultancy Services Company as well as throughout thereafter. My gratitude to K. G. Dewan, Sadiq Shafiq, Boben Anto and Rakesh Mishra whose ever helping hand remained a sustainable strength to me.

Grateful thanks to M/s BLUE ROSE PUBLISHESERS PRIVATE LIMITED, the Publishers without whose cooperation, guidance and advice, this book wouldn't have reached the readers.

Thanks to my friends, relatives and my family members. Their suggestions and support were a great strength for me in completing this book.

January 15, 2024 Prahalad Rao

LIFE IS TO LIVE TOGETHER

Mata Bhumih Putroham Prithivyah, Earth is my mother; I am her son - ~ Atharva Veda, 12-1-12 - "Nature has placed mankind under the governance of two sovereign masters, pain and pleasure. It is for them alone to point out what we ought to do, as well as to determine what we shall do." - Jerren Gan – Published in ILLUMINATION – DEC 19, 2022

Human takes birth on MOTHER EARTH RAREST OF THE RARE TIMES as told by Great Saints and their Holy Scripts of each Faith through Civilizations. The process of life bears the truth of the godly belief. One has to see around when he or she stands, how different Faiths in different languages, words, colors and so on, the beauty of which lies within one's looks how serene and strong they appeal the viewers that is what the past generations passed on, the present generation is witnessing and future generations will continue to witness. This is well understood if this much is understood that ultimately sums up Life is to Live Together. The congregation of the Faiths and understanding that generates a zeal to live together. Famous Families in the world including our own country lived by their names and bequeathed what they had to the next generation to remind them that those names are not ordinary names but made up of the unity and strength they practiced, withstood and safely handed over to their lineages. This exists in every Faith. The lineages proudly exhibit them holding in their hands that shake their minds how it was so prideful to symbolize them. This started with families, then the society and the nation. Let us try for a moment what I am writing here how it reflects within me, my family, my society and my nation. The concept of Life is to live together may not be a wayward but one that absorbs them in oneness withstanding the testing times. It would continue to hold on to hopes of generations to come, that being the tested stone.

"You should look at certain walls stained with damp, or at stones of uneven color. If you have to invent some backgrounds you will be able to see in these the likeness of divine landscapes, adorned with mountains, ruins, rocks, woods, great plains, hills and valleys in great variety; and expressions of faces and clothes and an infinity of things which you will be able to reduce to their complete and proper forms. In such walls the same thing happens as in the sound of bells, in whose stroke you may find every named word which you can imagine." - Leonardo da Vinci

What Mark Twain thought about 'The real reason why you were born': "There are two great days in a person's life - the day we are born and the day we discover why." Have you ever wondered if there is a concealed, mystifying and gigantic reason for which God decided to send you on Earth? God created each of us for a reason - and I think we can be the happiest when we are living in harmony with the purpose he has given us. But we need to know what it is…". What Maya Angelou said "One isn't necessarily born with courage, but one is born with potential? Without courage, we cannot practice any other virtue with consistency. We can't be kind, true, merciful, generous, or honest." What Virgin Group says: Togetherness is a hugely important aspect of life. It unites us, gives us security, much-needed support and a sense of belonging, and encourages us to love one another. What Henry Ford said: "Coming Together is a Beginning; Keeping Together Is Progress; Working Together Is Success. What John Lennon/Yoko Ono said: "A Dream You Dream Alone Is Only A Dream. A Dream You Dream Together Is Reality." What Mother Teresa said "I Can Do Things You Cannot, You Can Do Things I Cannot; Together We Can Do Great Things."

The thread that is passing through in all these lines in the writings stated before is being together, the opposite of which is individualized that incorporates quarrelsomeness. Online Free Dictionary defines this word as 'an inclination to be quarrelsome and contentious contentiousness disagreeableness - an ill-tempered and offensive disposition...'

In togetherness, one has to be true oneself, open minded and straight forward approach. These qualities concretize one's faith and trust in each other, the essential symbol and star mark of human life and guide towards strengthening further the relationship in each other, as a long standing stone in vertical form in a devastated civilization; the strength and spirit of the standing stone did not undergo any change rather made people of the generations get attracted and visit it once in lifetime so that it reminds one not to act as a moving basket but a strongly held one in one's hand at all the times which is the inner strength of humans to stand together, live together and love together; the Togetherness rather than accusing each other, bickering against each other and ultimately self-annihilating each other.

What for we are living without togetherness; it is like living in a desert bereft of any vegetation and continue to search for water to survive. Even the other living beings on Mother Earth know this cardinal concern of the life. God never made nor would make divisions among the humans; HE, rather wants humans to sink the divisions when one can see the original sense of humanity manifested by God in every human and other living beings. That is how the civilizations survived and generations lived.

The history also reminds us the destructive, debased character and animosity among some of the rulers in the world that also include our own country. Where do they stand today? When we read the history books when we were children and what the children of today are also reading understood and continues to understand the devilish acts of such rulers who not only destroyed and attempting to destroy even today a sense of belongingness among each other and continue to create more and more divisions politically, religiously and maritally, the sole purpose of which being to 'DIVIDE AND RULE', as an effective weapon in hand ignoring that that very weapon would destroy the same people who created or creating them, the end of humanity among the humans God has bestowed in every human born on Mother Earth. All this happens when the humans try to pierce the sword of hatredness for divisioning among the humans, most of whom are the victims of denial of a simple living being on Mother Earth. Today as well, it has become a namesake word for upbringing of the downtrodden community but the reality reflects different in the mirror when the politicians and the religious leaders see their faces in the mirror which is true to its character to be real and show to those humans who see it what reality stands for.

This human culprit has also entrenched in the families and societies in the country. Showmanship has become of greater importance as against simple minded and service oriented. There are also family members who are engaged in search for the best tools for divisioning the families including marital and societies in order to enjoy the maddened dancing joy forgetting that such joy is born through the sense of self cheating and injecting it in the families and societies. Those who held the family and societal values with great respect for generations are washed out because of rushing in them the highest order of selfishness and bigotry. Thus born the divisioning ill will among the families and societies. They caused deepest injury in the given environment like the wild fire in the forests burning whatever came in the way. The sensible people in the families including marital and societies realized the highly explosive situation developing in the families and societies and put their front foot forward to resist such move to the extent of their capability and strength and when failed, gave up and burnt themselves in the spreading wild fire. This is how the families including marital and societies which grew sometime or the other like flowers in the house garden together and collectively spreading the perfume of oneness. A flower whether small or big in size never considers as different from each other, the essence of which makes them grow together against all the oddities. This doctrine of Common Sense is twisted by the humans according to the times and opportunities thrown open up to them.

Today, we are searching for ways and means on how to disintegrate the togetherness so that the disintegrating humans could find excuse to seize the individualized, isolated spots in the families that includes marital and societies as readymade material to exploit individually and collectively to create social boiling in the society which is rather they find it difficult where the communities are integrated which are like the civilizational stones stated before standing not accessible for mutation and destruction. The historical events witnessed even the mutation and destruction when the foreigners invaded in different parts of the world including our own country. An historical wrong done by the invaders necessitates correcting it when the humans who suffered worst events caused by the invaders reunite and endeavour to restore the originality that existed.

This is considered as unjustifiable by a certain section of the people considering as if what had been done in the past was in order and refuse to reconcile with the reality that starts unmasking the injuries inflicted in the past rather than realizing the fact what was done was a fact and what is being done is also to set right the wrongs done in the past, also of necessity and fact. Such understanding dawns a new era among the humans that drives towards maintaining oneness and togetherness rather than trying to push forward wrong done as right that invites newer kinds of fiercely attacks using the weapon of disintegration in every given situation. This is anti-thesis of togetherness and integrated families and societies. Is there any limit for such acts if we don’t consider it call a spade as a spade? "Call a spade a spade" is a figurative expression. It refers to calling something "as it is"—that is, by its right or proper name, without "beating about the bush", but rather speaking truthfully, frankly, and directly about a topic, even to the point of bluntness or rudeness, and even if the subject is considered coarse, impolite, or unpleasant. Wikipedia

"............Philosopher Mircea Eliade proposed a reflection about the "Mother Earth". He compared Earth to the mother, on a symbolic level. Just like the mother, it is the first object of attachment that we encounter in the objective world. Earth holds us like a mother, it nurtures us like a mother does, providing food, chemicals, wood, and answering our every need in a seemingly omnipotent way, akin to the vision an infant has of its all-powerful mother until it has grown enough to fend for itself.

Moreover, clinical experience has demonstrated instances when patients separated from their homeland (immigrant workers, refugees, nomads) exhibit symptoms of depression and anxiety, echoing the situation of a child deprived of its mother's care. The similarity comes from the feeling of abandonment from the loss of a familiar, known, secure, gratifying object.

Psychoanalyst Melanie Klein theorized, from her observation of babies, that an infant at some stage fears that it has "damaged" its mother by clinging to her and feeding off her, and this causes the child to enter a phase of depression subsequent to so much guilt. This guilt actually allows us to mature enough and form a psyche that can both withstand frustration and develop an ability to feel remorse.

Are we moved enough by the plight of the planet to question ourselves to deal with depression and make amends at the same time?

This would mean that guilt and the ensuing need to "repair" are experienced at the very early moments of our life. While these theories are quite controversial, the central message is that humankind is capable of developing a stable psyche because of our very deep capacity to feel bad about our actions, and to delve into a more "gentle" identity and accept to make amends by learning, by "being good", and then by repairing the damage we have caused. As children, we thrive on a "good enough mother", rather than an all-powerful mother, and the guilt from damaging the mother, by claiming too much from her — in another form of all-powerfulness — is one step towards socialization and the integration of norms and values.

In practice, it is often very apparent in adults how many of their everyday actions have a source in their early interactions with their mothers. In regard to Earth, this is something that is quite apparent too: we do feel deeply moved by the consequences of our use of Earth and our all-powerfulness towards her.

One main question remains though: are we moved enough by the plight of the planet to question ourselves, deal with depression and make amends at the same time? If we are not, we should think of ways to allow ourselves to be moved by those feelings so familiar and yet so terrifying because they force us to confront the possibility that we are in fact powerless and our ultimate fear of becoming victims of something we cannot control at all — the revenge of she who created and fed, and on whom we depend for everything………" [Source: Humanity's Attachment to Mother Earth - 011•04•15 Oumar Konare [Our World Website]

Paul Bloom, a Canadian American psychologist said 'Crying is also triggered by opposites. You might cry on the worst day of your life and on the best. Weddings and funerals; the thrill of victory and the agony of defeat.'

One may wonder why I selected the title of the book as 'LIFE IS TO LIVE TOGETHER', the subject that humans are aghast in practical life, families are broken and husband and wife separated leaving the children to hang on in life. That is true as it is happening in reality of life, so one cannot call it an illusion. This aspect is dealt in more detail in the later part of this book. This book endeavoured to devote more on the subject of married life, entry of ego in such life cultivating a self-proclaiming order of life which can be beneficial as well as baneful and painful. These two factors that rule the married life are self-made for the superiority over each other; forgetting in that process the very purpose of marriage and married life and the beneficial interests of the offspring whose development and growth solely depends upon the serenity and sacredness of the relationship that existed between wife and husband. There are new branches of marriage [Example, Live-in-Partners and Live Apart Together - LAT] that have started giving birth among the individuals and adverse and consequential ill-effects in the society that have surpassed the cruellest treatment including murders on one or the other pretext. The States are engaged in making new laws and rules today to deal with such relationships. This is also dealt in details while dealing about the married life also dealt in the later part.

Plato's Cave: Do You Know the Difference between Reality and Illusion? - By Kenneth Samples - March 25,

2014 posted on Reasons Believe Website that one should know to differentiate them. It reads as follows:

"The great Greek philosopher Plato (427–347 BC) famously illustrated the difference between reality and illusion through a story about men who lived all their life in a cave. In Plato's allegory, these men were chained to pillars and could see only shadow cast on the cave's back wall by a fire that burned behind them, out of sight.

The men in the cave took great pride in their eyesight and in their interpretive abilities—yet all the time they were looking at shadows, mere illusions. Then, one of the men breaks out of the chains and makes it outside of the cave where he discovers a whole new world. When he reenters the cave to tell his friends about his marvelous epiphany they reject and resent him to the point of wanting to kill him.

Of course, there are several important philosophical lessons to be mined from Plato's cave allegory, one being the fact that a real metaphysical world exists independent of human experience and observation (what Plato called the world of the "Forms"). But Plato also intended his story to illuminate the life of his teacher, Socrates (470–399 BC), who was killed by the Athenian government for challenging ancient Greece's view of truth and reality.........

Reflections on Plato's Story

Personally, I find Plato's story disconcerting, if not downright haunting. Consider its application on three levels.

First, on an individual basis, it is easy to sleepwalk through life, especially for those born into privilege (like many of us living in the Western world). Many people accept the norms and categories they have been given without asking the truly deep questions of life.

Family upbringing, the media, school, and other cultural factors shape our practical worldview narrative of life. And these life narratives often point us toward goals of personal pleasure (sensualism), financial affluence (materialism), and prestige (egoism). These narratives and their end goals stand in stark contrast with the Christian [Author adds: and in all other Faiths] worldview narrative, which encourages the pursuit of truth, goodness, and beauty.

Second, as Plato no doubt intended, the message of this powerful allegory also challenges our political thinking. It is amazingly easy to accept a political ideology, especially when we talk only to people who agree with us. Unfortunately, in that case, we fail to benefit from hearing the best argument from the other political side and there is an absence of much-needed checks and balances.

Third, it seems to me that Plato's story challenges committed Christians as well. Believers in Christ must exercise a reasonable faith by appropriately putting their beliefs to the test. A faith seeking understanding should replace blind faith. God's gift of the life of the mind is meant to safeguard us against an undiscerning and excessively dogmatic religiosity. [Author adds: This is the intent in all other Faiths].

If this article and its content trouble you in one of the three ways discussed above, then I'm not alone in my philosophical angst. I know philosophical angst isn't easy to live with—but it's much better than living in a dark cave."

Togetherness gives us the strength and support we need to succeed. It allows us to come together and accomplish great things that would otherwise be impossible. Working together is essential for success, both in our personal lives and in our professional lives. Dozens of studies have shown that people who have social support from family, friends, and their community are happier, have fewer health problems, and live longer. Conversely, a relative lack of social ties is associated with depression and later-life cognitive decline, as well as with increased mortality.

Togetherness births when there is a sense of love among the people, the families and the wife and husband. The word love itself so complex it makes sometimes to subject it to minute test for psychological satisfaction whether the love one is tempted to is true or mimicker love. The word love is like a flower of different colours and different smells that leads one to think which one of them the best? Believing a particular is best, one bewilders later that that flower looked more beautiful but its smell not matching with its beauty. Here comes the real problem. How to match the beauty and smell of the flower which depends upon one who knows the art of matching of beauty and smell of flower? Even so, when flower starts drying up, its beauty also diminishes, yet, the flower continues to spread its original smell. In fact, such differentiation could be considered as discriminatory for; all the flowers are also born on Mother Earth, each having its most beautifying qualities, just as humans who are also born on Mother Earth. We are inclined to apply the test as in the case of flowers as humans by necessity of our negativity as we are used to do so ourselves to other humans. Thus, the basic understanding is also ignored by the humans.

The Purity of Love is thus explained:

"WHEN OVER THE YEARS SOMEONE HAS SEEN YOU AT YOUR WORST, AND KNOWS YOU WITH ALL YOUR STRENGTHS AND FLAWS, YET COMMITS HIM- OR HERSELF TO YOU WHOLLY, IT IS A CONSUMMATE EXPERIENCE. TO BE LOVED BUT NOT KNOWN IS COMFORTING BUT SUPERFICIAL. TO BE KNOWN AND NOT LOVED IS OUR GREATEST FEAR. BUT TO BE FULLY KNOWN AND TRULY LOVED IS, WELL, A LOT LIKE BEING LOVED BY GOD. IT IS WHAT WE NEED MORE THAN ANYTHING. IT LIBERATES US FROM PRETENSE, HUMBLES US OUT OF OUR SELF-RIGHTEOUSNESS, AND FORTIFIES US FOR ANY DIFFICULTY LIFE CAN THROW AT US." - TIM KELLER – AUTHOR - THE MEANING OF MARRIAGE

I consider it useful to acquaint the readers with the values, virtues and rigors of life that incorporated in a newly born child. As the child grows, whether it continues to carry those values and virtues is a matter that depends upon the parents to preserve and protect them within the growing child. Also, first to understand what is life and its purpose on Mother Earth after the human is born through the womb of mother. There is hardly any time for many of us to think about them and understand their depth and width on Mother Earth. Every human needs to know them to survive and sustain his or her life on Mother Earth. They are integral part of human but getting disintegrated day by day in the wake of hurriedness the humans want to live. [Definitions of hurriedness. overly eager speed (and possible carelessness) synonyms: haste, hastiness, hurry, precipitation - types: abruptness, precipitance, precipitancy, precipitateness, and precipitousness, suddenness. the quality of happening with headlong haste or without warning]. They do come to know them as the life process proceeds, some understand and others ignore them; those who understood them realize at one or other time of the life while those who continue to ignore them live in a state of abysmal depth of ignorance self-denying the meaning and purpose of life. **"THE GREATEST WEALTH IS TO LIVE CONTENT WITH LITTLE"-PLATO.**

I searched for meaning of 'Life' on Google Website. All talk about the purpose of the life but not its origin. Does this mean word 'Life' is indefinable? I am not a scholar, in any form one ordinarily assumed either in Sanskrit or Arabic or English or any other language for that matter. A humble human being born in a tiny village, endeavoured all through the life to live unassuming and egoless and continued to practice them throughout my life. What is unassuming and egoless?

LIFE IS 'SOUL. The womb is the organ in the body of a woman in which a baby develops before birth; the movements of the baby inside womb signal the manifestation of the Soul. In the time of Aristotle, it was widely believed that the human Soul entered the forming body at 40 days (male embryos) or 90 days (female embryos), and quickening was an indication of the presence of a Soul. The process is beyond human comprehension that is where we think of 'GOD'. This is the TRUTH AND ONLY THE TRUTH. SOME HUMANS ASK WHERE GOD IS. HUMANS FAIL TO UNDERSTAND THAT THE ANSWER TO THE QUESTION LIES WITHIN THE QUESTION. HOW? A HUMAN ASKING SUCH QUESTION WOULDN'T HAVE ASKED THAT WITHOUT THERE BEING 'SOUL' WITHIN HIM OR HER, THAT IS, WITHOUT SOUL, THE BODY DOESN'T MOVE. I do not know who is God because I have not seen Him in my eighty seven years of life but has been hearing a lot about God all around in different languages, in different moods, in different methods, in different attitudes, in different writings, in different speeches, musical [vocal and instrumental], articles written in different magazines, newspapers and so on, as presented in different electronic medias, as manifested in different Temples, Mosques, Churches, as told by the parents, as told by the highly learned and so on. There is, yet, an unanswered question that needs to be answered. The Path that is open to humans to Perceive God. This Path is available to everyone but what is not available is to understand that. Though I have not seen God, as stated before but I experience the God and truly believe so doing daily what Great Saints and Sages believed and follow the Path they left behind for the humans to know about God. This thinking is limited to me because I cannot assume an authoritative position in that respect being also an ordinary humble human. Nevertheless, there are humans in the world including our own country who experience God through their own way of living life and find the presence of God within that experience.

Introducing Bhaj Govindum composed by Sri Adi Shankara and sung by M.S. Subbalakshmi; Dr. S. Radhakrishnan {a great Philosopher and former President of India} noted that "Ray of Knowledge and Bhakti are one and the same. When Knowledge lodges securely in mind, it becomes Wisdom. When Wisdom is integrated with Life and shoots out into action, it becomes Bhakti. Knowledge when matures is Bhakti. If the Knowledge does not transform into Bhakti, such Knowledge is useless. To believe Bhakti and Knowledge are different from each other is ignorance." Knowledge is theoretical while Bhakti is practical. Bhakti is to translate the knowledge in actuality when the knowledge attains fruitfulness. What one wants to achieve in one's life through his or her bestowed knowledge is possible only when that knowledge is encompassed with the devotional commitment that is a sincere and honest effort to earn that which one wants to achieve in life and, that devotion and commitment is Bhakti. Sincerity and honesty are the integral part of Bhakti and Bhakti {Shraddha} is to centralize the entire energy in concentration and it is that concentration that enables one to create something perceivable but not visible, that is, GOD. This opens up the Path to pursue the intrinsic strength within to get spiritualization from the Soul within. The human thus derives the intrinsic strength with positivity in mind and all actions with positivity have the protection shield from the Soul.

Shraddha is faith and bhakti is devotion, the first is prerequisite to follow the latter. That is, bhakti has no purpose without the faith. First faith should manifest in mind and then move towards bhakti. Example, I have faith in something that establishes firmness of that something in my mind. Then, I want to feel or perceive that something. It is bhakti or devotion that takes me towards my aspiration to feel or perceive about what is that something. Once I find myself immense satisfaction I have felt or perceived from that something, I make that bhakti as part of my life. Committed devotion thus followed creates the power of concentration through the process of centralizing the energy.

In other words, the power of concentration always helps to maintain positivity in mind and protects it from entry of negativity, the aim of which is to keep the mind in turbulence. Let us see its application in practical life. We ordinarily believe worship is confined only to a particular object of faith in religious terms whereas in every action or work we do in life, such action or work can fructify only when we accord the same sense of worship we do for our object of faith. It is also said that object of faith is ingrained in each and every part of our daily life thus suggesting that since the object of faith is present in action and work; our action or work should be done with a total sense of devotion. It is that devotion in our action and work that makes one free from fear or apprehension, thus generating the self-confidence and self-conviction which has the capacity to make one to attain the level of contentment in proficiency in the subject matter one is engaged in and continues to enhance it corresponding to one's commitment and devotion. That is why it is also known that 'Work is Worship'. Having made up the faith, the object of bhakti has to be practiced in every work or action. Such person, who has integrated such practice in daily life, having faith the same object of faith is present in act and work, produces the best quality of thoughts and products embodying therein the depth of the proficiency and fearlessness.

Let me also say few words about the 'other livings or co-livings' on Mother Earth. The Soul is not manifested only in humans, also in all the other living beings. They don't have the Consciousness {though research is in progress to establish the presence of Consciousness also among the other living beings} but do have 'Conscience" that is demonstrated through their love, affection and kindness towards humans when humans consider them as their equal partners and show them the same love, affection and kindness. They are countless while humans are countable and, most of them, if not all of them, provide comfort to humans in one form or the other.

Mother Earth is the creation of the Creator and not the humans. The humans are also one of the living beings on Mother Earth, always in minority compared to other species; yet humans want to prevail upon rather than protecting them that occur because of increasing degradation in the human values and virtues and ingredients of natural law Mother Earth enforces the order of living on every living being including humans. Such differentiation among the humans leads to continuing conflicts between the humans and the other living beings. The pain human feels when there is an injury is also felt by all other living beings whenever injury is caused to them. When selfishness exceeds its extremity on the part of the humans, reactions from other living beings begin in one form or the other; example is the pandemic we witnessed recently. This is so because humans want to impose more and more unequal treatment to them even they also being equal partners, there being Soul also in them. When this happens, the Nature is forced to intervene to correct the imbalance due to acts against the natural laws existing on Mother Earth. One may ask, do all other living beings show the same spirit to humans? They do except where humans create provocative circumstances and make to them to fight in self-defence, also for survival.

God is unknown to the eyes of all beings on Mother Earth. Soul is the embodiment of God, the only Absolute Truth, not visible but resides invisibly in the Soul or the Self and emanates in the form of spirit. For all beings on earth, death is the only Truth that happens when Soul or the Self leaves the body on the earth. What humans experience pleasure and pain on earth is in material and spiritual forms, in most cases, in material form. It is also true that humans, most of them, believe in God and lead a life of materialism and spiritualism, the extent the circumstances permit. All other beings on earth live in their own natural ways not knowing materialism and spiritualism; they do experience pleasure and pain which is understood by their own way of communication among each other in expressionless term, also noticeable by humans. The elements of pleasure and pain are the parts of the materialistic way of living of humans because of physical sensitiveness the mind and body present. It is not to suggest here that one should give up materialistic living and live like a Sanyasi. It is not that. Practicing Shraddha [Bhakti] is more relevant and important for those living in worldly affairs than a Sanyasi. Because, one could learn how controlled materialistic world one can lead. One should also learn how to prevail over the mind through the practice Quietitudeness. Quietitudeness also helps controlling and self-treatment of Blood Pressure,

Sugar (to prevent Diabetes), positive breathing system very vital for the functioning of the body and mind, increasing positivity that also helps control growth of chronic diseases. Above all, quietened mind makes human to live in peace or do in peace whatever one wants or supposed to do as part of profession, duty, activity, business etc.

As humans, we consider we have strength and ability to fight for some causes, good or bad depending upon what occurs in one's mind, also to fight among ourselves for one reason or the other, where the situations become so necessary to show our superiority of strength, as also to struggle with life to earn and live with dignity of life. That shows we have the strongest strength to stand up to face such situations in life. Where that strength goes out of us once we develop some signal of weakness or nervousness to which we become victim rather than victor using our God given strength, reasoning and ascertainment to search for positivity within us, the birth of which itself is the beginning of the self-treatment of such fixations in mind. One may say all this is nonsense. Author accepts this with humility. Let us take an example. One while driving his or her car on the road when happens to meet with an accident, he or she get perplexed with anxiety and trauma taking place inside. If such an accident causes some minimal or ordinary injury to the body or some damage to the car, both are curable which fact does not occur to him or her at that moment, what occurs is loss of thinking power and strength in the body? This is the critical moment in one's life that one should lean towards positivity than the negativity. That leads to self-understanding, self-confidence and self-development.

Swami Vivekananda's Thoughts on Self Confidence

- Faith, faith, faith in ourselves and faith in God – this is the secret of greatness. If you have faith in all the three hundred and thirty millions of your mythological gods, and still have no faith in yourselves, there is no salvation for you.
- What makes the difference between man and man is the difference in this Shraddha (faith) and nothing else. What makes one man great and another weak and low is this Shraddha.
- The remedy for weakness is not brooding over weakness, but thinking of strength. Teach men of strength that is already within them.
- You must not say that you are weak. How do you know what possibilities lie behind that degradation on the surface? You know but little of that which is within you. For behind you is the ocean of infinite power and blessedness.
- We can overcome the difficulty by constant practice. We must learn that nothing happen to us, unless we make ourselves susceptible to it.
- It is the coward and the fool who says, "This is fate" – so says the Sanskrit proverb. But it is the strong who stands up and says, "I will make my fate". It is people who are getting old who talk of fate. Young men generally do not come to astrology.
- You have in you a thousand times more than is in all the books. Never lose faith in yourself; you can do anything in this universe. Never weaken, all power is yours.

- You have to grow from the inside out. None can teach you, none can make you spiritual. There is no other teacher but your own Soul.
- You cannot believe in God until you believe in yourself.

All this leads us towards one direction- Action is Life and Inaction is Death. Positivity is life and negativity is distress and depression, leading sometimes to suicide.

"Suicide/Depression – the future epidemic – Shri Ramakrishna and Swami Vivekananda on suicide" posted on 19th July, 2013 by Sandeep Kodam (Extracts):

Swami Vivekananda on suicide:

"THE FIRST THING IS NOT TO HATE OURSELVES."

................You will generally hear that this Vedanta, this philosophy and other Eastern systems, look only to something beyond, letting go the enjoyments and struggle of this life. This idea is entirely wrong. It is only ignorant people, who do not know anything of Eastern thought, and never had brain enough to understand anything of its real teaching, that tell you so. On the contrary, we read in our scriptures that our philosophers do not want to go to other worlds, but depreciate them as places where people weep and laugh for a little while only and then die. As long as we are weak we shall have to go through these experiences; but whatever is true, is here, and that is the human soul. And this also is insisted upon, that by committing suicide, we cannot escape the inevitable; we cannot evade it. But the right path is hard to find. The Hindu is just as practical as the Western, only we differ in our views of life......................."

Togetherness is strength and individualization or disintegrating is extreme weakness. Once we take a human form or personhood having come out of the womb of the mother, life within wants to convert itself into action in one form or the other depending upon the choice of the human and that makes one to search for further pursuit and means for survival for oneself and for other humans on Mother Earth whose blessing is to co-exist to exist. All that what humans do during his or her life time is the purpose for which he or she is born on Mother Earth; those who engage their life in doing goodness for humans and other living beings on Mother Earth, the return one receives back is exhilarating that appeals and absorbs in the Consciousness as well as, more importantly, in the Conscience that is attached adjunct to the Soul, such person having put his or her best efforts to sacrifice to serve others both in terms of humans and other living beings, before self.

GOOD WORDS AND DEEDS REMAIN BEHIND US WHEN WE DEPART FROM MOTHER EARTH, ACCUMMULATE THEM AS MANY AS ONE CAN WHILE ON MOTHER EARTH FOR; THEY ARE THE ORNAMENTS WE WILL BE WEARING WHILE LEAVING MOTHER EARTH AND PEOPLE FOR WHOM WE HAVE SAID GOOD WORDS AND DONE GOOD DEEDS REMEMBER US FOR EVER, THEIR WISHES ARE CONVEYED TO "ALMIGHTY.

One may also ask where was the need for me to go through all that I have stated before. Question is relevant and my answer is when one wants to know more and more about oneself, he or she get encaged in self-denying the opportunity to be also in touch with others and know them to learn and enlarge the knowledge that offer innumerable benefits to live together happily and peacefully on Mother Earth and progress and prosper through the process of mutuality to mutually benefit and enjoy the life.

Let us now revert to essence of Life and its incense [a gum, spice, or other substance] that is burned for the sweet smell it produces: “the sharp lingering sweetness of incense". Today, this is produced in various forms and used for various purposes and occasions. Attribution of Life to incense is that when Life comes on Mother Earth in human form incorporates in itself a kind of incense, smelling of which spreads sweetness all around, more so, among humans who being the superior gene on earth not only enjoy that smell, also to like that incense in their relationship with other living beings which though lack consciousness, yet enjoy the reflection of humans enjoying the sweet smell of incense. If a pet dog or cat in one’s home looks at its master using various kinds of perfumes that pervade with sweet smell also equally share it but cannot express. As the humans know various purposes for which they use the incense filled environment on different occasions, so also, the other living beings look towards the humans to convey that sweetness towards them, that suggests love and kindness enriched in the sweet smell make them more nearer to and comfortable with humans. Humans need to consider such approach or attitude as their duty or obligation towards other living beings that is what Mother Earth contemplates. This begs much more among the married humans for; the sweet smell compels both enjoy and encompasses meaning of love and kindness towards each other. That raises the question – what is married Life?

The Definition of Marriage

Marriage is the union of a man and a woman, forming a social and legal contract, union of a man and a woman. Marriage commonly means the intimate and equal partnership between a man and a woman. This bond, often seen as divine in nature, mirrors the relationship God shares with his Temple or Mosque or Church or as contemplated in Holy Scripts. Not just physical, this union extends to emotional and spiritual realms, acting as an emblem of connection on multiple levels. The depth of this bond is marked by key elements such as fair fighting, acceptance, appreciation, and healthy communication channels that keep it thriving.

A social and legal contract

Marriage is more than just a loving relationship between two individuals. It is also a social and legal contract that binds them together in various ways. When two people enter into marriage, they are making a commitment not only to each other but also to society as a whole. This contract provides certain rights and responsibilities, including financial support, inheritance rights, and decision-making authority. Additionally, marriage creates a sense of stability and order within the community by establishing clear rules and expectations for couples. It serves as the foundation for families and contributes to the overall well-being of individuals and society. Marriage is not only about love and companionship; it is also an agreement that carries legal implications. Couples who get married often have their union recognized by law, with specific requirements regarding consent, age restrictions, and documentation. This legal aspect ensures that both partners have certain protections under the law in case of disputes or dissolution of the marriage. Furthermore, being part of this social contract brings benefits such as tax advantages, health insurance coverage eligibility through spouses' plans, and access to shared resources like joint bank accounts or property ownership.

The Purpose of Marriage

Marriage serves the purpose of creating a lifelong partnership, building a family, providing emotional and financial support, and fostering companionship and love. Creating a lifelong partnership Marriage is about more than just a wedding ceremony; it is the foundation of a lifelong partnership. This union involves two individuals committing to each other in good times and bad, for better or worse. It is a sacred bond that requires love, trust, and mutual respect. Through marriage, couples create a sense of stability and security as they navigate life's challenges together. They form a deep connection built on companionship, shared goals, and emotional support. A strong partnership allows couples to grow closer over time, strengthening their relationship and creating a solid foundation for the future.

Building a family

Building a family is one of the main purposes of marriage. It involves creating a stable and loving environment to raise children. Through marriage, couples commit themselves to providing emotional and financial support for their family members. They work together as partners to nurture their children, fostering personal growth and fulfillment within their family unit. Building a family within the context of marriage helps to create strong bonds and connections among its members, promoting a sense of belonging and love that lasts a lifetime.

Emotional and financial support

Marriage provides both emotional and financial support to couples. In times of joy or sorrow, spouses can rely on each other for comfort and understanding. The emotional bond created through marriage allows partners to share their thoughts, feelings, and experiences, knowing that they have someone who will listen without judgment. This emotional support fosters a sense of security and strengthens the relationship. Financially, marriage often brings stability as couples pool their resources together. Sharing expenses such as housing costs, utilities, groceries, and healthcare can alleviate financial burdens and provide a stronger foundation for the family unit. Additionally, many married couples enjoy benefits such as joint bank accounts or shared insurance policies that offer greater financial protection.

Companionship and love

Marriage provides a deep sense of companionship and love. When two people join in matrimony, they commit to supporting and caring for each other throughout their lives. This bond offers emotional intimacy and the opportunity to build a strong connection with one's spouse. Love within marriage is not just about romantic feelings; it also encompasses mutual respect, trust, and understanding.

Companionship forms the foundation of a thriving marriage, as it allows couples to share their joys, sorrows, dreams, and challenges together. It is through this companionship that couples can navigate life's ups and downs with unwavering support from their partner.

Love in marriage goes beyond just romance—it involves unconditional acceptance and genuine affection for one another. It strengthens the emotional connection between spouses by fostering empathy, compassion, and forgiveness. In a loving marriage relationship, both partners continuously nurture their bond by expressing care and appreciation for each other every day. The love shared between husband and wife creates an environment where they can grow individually while still finding comfort in knowing that they have a constant source of support right beside them. [Source: marry on chain website]

In Hinduism, the marriage (Sanskrit: vivaha, romanized: Vivāha, lit. 'Marriage') is the most important of all the samskaras, the rites of passage described in the Dharamshastras texts: [1]

"Variously defined, it is generally described to be a social institution for the establishment and regulation of a proper relationship between the sexes, as stated by Manu. Marriage is regarded to be a sacrament by Hindus, rather than a form of social contract, since they believe that all men and women are created to be parents, and practise dharma together, as ordained by the Vedas.[2] The Brahmanas state that a man is only said to be "complete" after marrying a woman, and acquiring progeny." [Source: Wikipedia]

In Islam, "THE COMING together of a man and a woman in marriage is one of the most unique events in the universe. All the things created in the universe are created in pairs, but the compatibility that exists between a man and a woman cannot be found in any other created thing. When a man and a woman come together as partners for life, it is evident that they have been made for each other through a conscious plan.

Marriage is not simply a social institution. In Islam, it has an importance far greater than this. According to the Islamic concept of life, God Almighty created an ideal world, Paradise. Paradise is a perfect and eternal world. God wants to select those women and men who may qualify to settle in this highly refined colony of Paradise. For the purpose of this selection or test, God provided men and women with free-will whilst settling them on Earth." [Spirit of Islam Website]

In Christianity, "for Christians of both the Orthodox and Roman Catholic Churches marriage is a sacrament. Through the prayers and actions of our wedding rites we profess the presence of Christ in the Spirit and believe that it is the Lord who unites a man and a woman in a life of mutual love. In this sacred union, husband and wife are called by Christ not only to live and work together, but also to share their Christian life so that each with the aid of the other may progress through the Holy Spirit in the life of holiness and so achieve Christian perfection. This relationship between husband and wife is established and sanctified by the Lord. As a sacred vocation, marriage mirrors the union of Christ and the church" (Eph. 5:23).

In Buddhism, "the Buddhist view of marriage considers marriage a secular affair and as such, it is not considered a sacrament. Buddhists are expected to follow the civil laws regarding marriage laid out by their respective governments. While the ceremony itself is civil, many Buddhists obtain the blessing from monks at the local temple after the marriage is completed." [Source: BuddhaSasana Home Page English Section]

In the Jain community, "marriage is an event of two people and two families. It is the parent's responsibility to introduce their children to a potential spouse. It can't be regarded as an arranged marriage because the couple is provided a long period to understand each other and take marriage decisions. When the couple is agreed, an engagement is organized. In this ceremony, symbolic gifts and items are exchanged between both families. It generally takes place in the community hall or the groom's residence"[Source: WEDGATE – Matrimonial Services Website]

In Sikhism, they are not said to be husband and wife who merely have physical contact only. Rather they alone are called husband and wife who have one soul in two bodies. Sri Guru Granth Sahib, p.788, Var Suhi.[Source: Sikh Missionary Society [U.K] Website]

That is what the most powerfully integrated relationship embedded in the word 'marriage'; this was there since the birth of the civilizations and would continue to be in every future civilizations. The ultimate of marriage is spiritual unionism blessed by God to men and woman living on Mother Earth. Fortunate are those whom God has bestowed the spiritualization of love between the man and woman to live together not to think apart from each other once that love is born through the marriage. It is the duty of married couple to come out of self-made prejudices once married that exists when each think independent of other that gives birth to egoistic outlook that divides the One into Two. There should not be any sense of ego once two souls merged into one and togetherness thus bound in life, if understood in its purity, provides a permanent place of oneness in life. Life is to live together, disregarding which leads to misery overtaking the pleasure in every walk of life which is the underlying depth of marriage that is ingrained with love, indescribable in length and width, for married men and woman. Its ignorance splits the love into two causing sometimes reparable but many times irreparable depending upon the level of negativity developed against each other.

In such situations, that is, where the married life lands itself into conflicts and confrontation necessitated on account of differential treatment among the couple whose Soul should be one though the bodies are two. Such treatment opens up when one starts thinking the other as not equal on one excuse or the other. Such sentiments are not made up of couple but grown up because differentiating the EGO, one claiming superiority over the other that is pestered by that ego. Ego is born out of the mind dominated by the negative thoughts and positivity is blackened or some other personal reasons and inklings. Once, these are acceded to, the entire frame of personality so doing changes and take a different course unknowing whether it is for good or bad.

Persistently pursing such attitude intensifies the burning sensation within and distancing in length and width of life.

None of the one among couple inclined to show some signs of the bright spot within oneself. That is, to understand that the Ego is not made by God but by human, God's desire towards humans, in fact, is that the married couple should be free from bondage of Ego. Where the situation reaches a stage of breakdown, the first duty of such couple is to think of the interests and future of the its just born child or growing children and that, at least, make them realize though what they intend is for each other's sake, they commit a sin when they ignore the welfare of the child or children born to the couple for; they know well that the child or children so born, have no independent capability or protection to grow without parental care. Side tracking this silver lining in the surrounded gloom suggests that the Ego in either of them is important than the child or the children who are standing before and staring at them. Where has the genesis of love and kindness towards such child or children gone out? Has it been burnt within the heart of the couple?

The ultimate parting of each other indicates so. Law is there to fill up the gaps in such life and about the custody of the child or children through the envisaged legal process. It needs to be appreciated that the mother and father are the two hands of the child or children, separation of which makes the child or children agonized, if not orphaned. Human knows the state of life without hand. Online Dictionary states 'Yet, when combined with the development of the human brain, the human hand has evolved to permit incredible function contributing to social, functional, and cultural importance. As with many aspects of anatomy, form is function. There is a plethora of orthopedic literature surrounding the anatomy of the human hand, its functions, and its pathology'. Are these facts not known to the parting couple? Or does the couple think to remain muted to the reality? These sensitive and sentimental feelings and concerns should arouse the couple before taking final step which itself also feels deeply disturbed but helpless to stop.

Such times are testing times in the life of the couple. One among them who cools down creating calmness within which is the one who shows sign of birth of Positivity that has the power to overthrow the egoistic attitudes and makes space for mutuality, the hallmark of the marriage and life and steps forward, in my view, is the most sacred minded one as if so nearer to the God or Goddess or Godly Qualities. Among the married couple in particular, when the signs of blinded scars appearing on each other's face, one who moves first to erase the scars is the one who won the world. Hesitation in either of them pulls back the spirit of positivity when the negativity regains its lost strength and places the couple in perplexities. There is no meaning in chasing a wrong path to find a right path knowing that the wrong path [negativity] is never interested to show the right path. Better course, instead, will, therefore, be to search the right path that is hidden in positivity and walk freely and fearlessly. Absence of intent to follow such course open either of the married couple drives back to a most pathetic condition that continues to intensify uncontrolled, the sign of birth of the breaking down point in life. Seize the positive opportunity given by God pushing back the negativity that is presently ruling the mind and move forward to reach each other to closeness.

Love is weightier than ornaments such as diamond and gold. The former is sharable mutually while the latter is saleable. The genesis love is humanness while the genesis of hatred is inhumanness. Love is God given while hatredness is man-made. Love is indestructible while hatred is like an infection which, unless cured properly and timely, continues to re-infect opening up space for chronic diseases in the body. The married couple is human and should uphold the essence and principles of humanity that ties up the couple tightly and guide towards prosperity and happier life. There is no medicine where love is infected; it is curable only through self-curing. Accord weightiest weight on love and, if that is followed, there is no space for hatredness in measuring scale. The ornaments sold are purchasable but love once separated remains so for ever. Even if reconnected, it will be like jointing the electric wire using the tape. It will lose its original shining because the suspicion once rooted in the mind is highly difficult to uproot it.

"God operates by different rules of time and space. And God's infinite greatness, which we would expect to diminish us, actually makes possible the very closeness that we desire." [Source: Celebrate Yoga Website]

All the Other Beings on Mother Earth live on God given relationship. Absence of this theme of life and love drives one into wilderness where one keeps moving but never settles in life. One may ask what is meaning of pain in life. If this does not exist in life, one will not be able to know what the pleasure is. The pleasure acquires a state of possession when one feels free from pain. If there were to be no pain in life, the pleasure loses its sense and essence in life. Philosophers have long appreciated the curious relationship between pain and pleasure. "Plato describes

Socrates rubbing his aching leg and saying, "How strange would appear to be this thing that men call pleasure! And how curiously it is related to what is thought to be its opposite, pain!' … Both pain and pleasure in life coexist. It is another matter as to why the humans undergo difficulties in life. This usually occurs when the negativity is accorded permanency in one's mind ignoring the fact that there is a source of pleasure also, that is, positivity, cultivation of which should be the sole object and spirit when two humans meet each other or when a man and woman get married. The character of negativity is to keep the humans breaking into pieces while positivity character is to assemble or reassemble the broken pieces and to bring back them to sense and feeling of oneness.

To my best understanding, the difficulties confront humans when human assumes more egoism that manifests the 'negativity' in the mind. Negativity never allows one to be free from difficulties when human is obsessed and merged in excessive egoism. These egoistic tendencies can result in exploitation, oppression, and aggression. People who meditate, or who have some practice that awakens presence, begin to experience a separation between their awareness and their egoistic selves. The humans use rein to control the horse; so also, negativity can be controlled applying rein in mental attitude. The challenge is, on most occasions, this decision is an unconscious one. The difference between positive and negative attitudes is the decision that someone has made on how they will respond to a situation they are facing. In its simplest form, attitude is nothing more than a decision that we make on how we respond to what is going on around us. Positive action – when someone chooses to respond positively to a situation, they tend to move into action mode or solution mode. They recognise they can't change the past and therefore the problem, but they can influence what happens next.

According to Bentham (1781), **"NATURE HAS PLACED MANKIND UNDER THE GOVERNANCE OF TWO SOVEREIGN MASTERS, PAIN AND PLEASURE. IT IS FOR THEM ALONE TO POINT OUT WHAT WE OUGHT TO DO, AS WELL AS TO DETERMINE WHAT WE SHALL DO."**

It's true that some of our ability to deal with hardships and failure has to do with biological traits and genetics. Some of it may have to do with luck. But mostly it has to do with the environment and people around us. Our parents, siblings, peers, educators, and community all play a vital role in shaping who we become.

Now, author wishes to touch his personal views gained through his life so far. Negativity of mind resulting, in many cases, into depression, calls for an earnest intervention by virtue of experience, witness to the sufferings, readiness to share other's sadness equally as of one's own, extending help of whatever kind and standing along invigorating spirit of positivity blinded by the negativity, helping those undergoing the torments of negativity and depression. All these are from those learned, researchers and spiritual leaders expressed through their writings for the benefit of those affected. I have presented them above being, in my view, prominently appealing and awakening. This is one part. Other part is translating them into reality by the humans having such problems in life and how best they make use of them. It doesn't end there. It ends when such humans should rebel against negativity imposed upon them to relieve from its pains. The word 'rebel' used invokes a sense of strong mental and physical strength to decisively fight the cause that shows a semblance of authoritarian and dictator in the governing system. Formation of negativity and depression in the mind may be one or many negative reasons happened or happening in one's life. One who has developed such formation in mind is more prone to accord importance and focus thereon which then assumes the character of an 'object' seeking always for focus either how to survive or how to get away. Recognition so attached to the object opens up a locked box having so much of hidden events of life that start flaming up with burning sensation in the mind and body. Swami Chinmayananda said that 'past is dead and is like carrying a dead body on one's shoulder that agitates the mind, future is frightening while the present is that in one lives.' Based on this, I submit that let us not recall the dreadful past nor think of frightening future. Live in the present and enjoy the life.

Negativity, according to my limited knowledge, occurs because of the circumstances. How one permits the negativity or what makes the negativity to enter into the mind and body. Body is the reflection of the mood of the mind – negative or positive. This is important to understand first. Negativity is born out of denial mode. This is not willing to accept the better part of life or refusal to listen a sane and sensible suggestion or advice, not willing to acknowledge the gratitude to someone who helped in certain situations, accumulating ideas unhelpful to the individual, floating in some thoughts believing them practical but not able to materialize them, always sitting in fixation on some or the other matter that doesn't exist or has become part of past, always brooding over the doubts on ability or capacity to do, feeling a sense of loss of faith, belief, confidence and control in oneself. All we do when we are captured by the negativity, we will be doing anything we do in a devil's workshop.

All these characters get settled in the mind start moving in the senses in the body leading to physical reactions and a sense of rejection of life. These characters are either forced upon in a given circumstance or caused due to inhuman and abusive treatment at some place or the other which severely hurts the person's sentiments. Let us understand that the negativity with the signs of the kind mentioned ordinarily does not come of its own. It is the result of a kind of treatment meted out in one's life within or outside the family and compels to loosing belief, faith, confidence, control, the foundations of the normal functional body and mind. That one who is thus subjected to finds him or her expressionless building up pressurising negative thoughts and communication within, there being none, as believed by him or her, to whom he or she could open up that helps ease the mental pressure. That further leads to loneliness most harmful to one's health and life. "The only time we waste is the time we spend thinking we are alone" - Mitch Albom.

Life is tough and we all have our own challenges to face. But we don't have to face them alone. With a caring heart and encouraging hand, we can all play a role in supporting others through their greatest hardships more so, in married life. [Life Is Tough: Overcoming Hardship and Failure – Kathryn Selfert. Ph.D. – Psychology Today]

In all acts in our life, increasing attachment is to the mind (Ego) that makes up our behavioural pattern in the society or in our work culture or in our relationships or in our outlook or in our biasness, or in our respects for others, in our readiness to listen to others and so on. This has become a way of our life. Why is it so? Gap between one's mind (ego) and the Soul one has built up in oneself subordinating the Soul to the ego. Ego in itself has no form and it postures its presence through human physical existence making that existence to believe as one and to feel the materialistic world as more important for living than anything else. This is where we get trapped in real life birthing increasing miseries, selfishness, insensibility, failures, depression leading sometimes to suicide, exuberance and excitement resulting in disastrous consequences and so on. Attitudes of this kind preoccupy with a sense of egoism prepared to take high risks and rashness unmindful of the harm these would cause to oneself and others. The persons of this nature don't think beyond their self-image and venture upon discarding the reality staring at the eyes. They disregard the signals of the inner voice [Conscience] against such adventurism. They scorn at any one advising them not to do such act. The cause for this is again the dominance of egoism bereft of reasoning and rationality. Mishaps, accidents, tragedies for families and kith and kin strike in most of these cases.

"Your mind can be your enemy or friend. If you always follow your heart, your mind will feel neglected. If you follow only your mind, your heart will never forgive you. Never ignore your conscience, yet always be conscious of reason. Make your heart and mind friends and you will have peace of mind throughout life's -

seasons." - — Suzy Kassem, Rise Up and Salute the Sun: The Writings of Suzy Kassem

Absence of God-fearing culture has become order of the day. This is evident from the types of mishaps and crimes are happening. (God-fearing used to describe religious people who try to obey the rules of their religion and to live in a way that is considered morally right). These are frightening and horrendous. The religious rules and the state laws have little or no concern for those committing such acts. Late APJ Abdul Kalam, former President once said "........ In India we only read about death, sickness, terrorism, crime. Why are we so NEGATIVE? Negativity has replaced the positivity in our thoughts and deeds."

Ana Nogales, Ph.D., is a clinical psychologist and well-known media personality, columnist, and speaker. A family therapy specialist, she is the author of Parents Who Cheat: How Children and Adults Are Affected When Their Parents Are Unfaithful, as well as Latina Power! Using 7 Strengths You Already Have to Create the Success You Deserve and Dr. Ana Nogales' Book of Love, Sex and Relationships. Dr. Nogales is also the Clinical Director of the non-profit organization that she founded, Casa de la Familia, established for victims of rape, sexual assault, child sexual and physical abuse, human trafficking, and domestic violence.

Dr. Nogales is also the Clinical Director of the non-profit organization that she founded, Casa de la Familia, established for victims of rape, sexual assault, child sexual and physical abuse, human trafficking, and domestic violence.

She wrote an Article in Psychology Today posted on website which emphatically encourages the youths to live their life to the fullest rather than develop frustration in life detrimental to one's own life. Excerpts from the Article which I consider as highly motivating:

1. Life is an invitation to learn. We can learn something from every moment, good or bad.
2. Life is not static; it's in constant movement, much like the waves of the ocean. Each wave that comes brings with it new experiences, and each one is different. Just as the bad waves can sometimes show no mercy, the good ones come along and refresh us. Nothing lasts forever.
3. Life is a gift; some people depart too soon and don't have the fortune to know life. Those who have it should enjoy it.
4. Our lives are not only our own. They also belong to those who surround us. We should take care of ourselves because we are important to others—even though we sometimes forget it.
5. Each new day is a new experience. If we don't live it, we won't know what we're missing.
6. We are the designers of our life. It is our challenge to find beauty, even—and especially—when the opposite occurs. Finding beauty in the world is possible and brings countless rewards.
7. We all live through experiences that leave scars. However, there is always someone to give us a hand during those difficult times. The important thing is to accept that help.
8. Making an effort to deal with problems can make us aware of how strong we really are. Life's

challenges don't exist only to upset us—they exist so that we understand ourselves better and get to know who we really are.

9. To live is to discover something about ourselves of which we were not aware.
10. To live is to look at ourselves in the mirror and discover a message of love in our own eyes.
11. To live is to allow ourselves to fall in love—with someone, with something, or with life itself.
12. Viewing death as a source of meaning can be comforting for many—but rather than using this as an argument in favour of suicide, it's critical to leverage such a perspective in order to make the most of life while it lasts.
13. Death is waiting for each of us anyway; why call on it before our time?

Ana Nogales has enwrapped the meaning of real life which engrosses every human. This spirit needs to be inculcated in the way of living of every human that embraces the Soul that offers more positivity to human thinking and enables to discard the negativity effects. Understanding of the essence of life as envisaged in the Article empowers all those self-caged into negativity and depression to wake up to the reality of life to enjoy as enjoyed by other humans on the earth. I earnestly believe that my efforts on elimination of negativity in thoughts and depression, among the humans, would be able to succeed in overcoming them. I consider it a greatest satisfaction and gratitude to those engaged in bringing succour to the affected ones.

There is another angle that invites anxiety, hopelessness, depression in the childhood and adolescence due to marital discord. Another angle for this is parental pressure on the teens and adolescents to excel in their examination, particularly, the Board, College and Competitive examinations. Third aspect is Lifestyles today have undergone sea change compared to what were there 30-40 years back.

This can be attributed to globalization, especially the stress and pressure that globalization is creating in the overall living environment. Technological advancement, part of globalization, has thrown innumerable usage systems in all walks of life, the excessive use of which is deeply disturbing the peace of mind in the families, teenagers and adolescents, the attachment having been increased manifold. Globalization, as one can understand, is the spread of products, technology, information, and jobs across national borders and cultures. In economic terms, it describes an interdependence of nations around the globe fostered through free trade. (Investopedia).

According to another source - It has been experienced that every step of movement towards economic, political and cultural modernization, taken by the state in India, is responded to by the people with an enhanced sense of self-consciousness and awareness of identity. Cultural modernization, sponsored by the forces of globalization, is resented if it encroaches upon or does not promote the core cultural values of society, its language, social practices and styles of life. The vigour of the renewed sense of self-awareness generated among the members of the local cultures and communities is such as to succeed in making adaptive reconciliation with the forces of globalization. The linkages both visible and invisible, defining the cultural interdependence among communities and regions in India which have existed historically, reinforce instead of threatening the national identity. These bonds seem to become stronger as India encounters the forces of modernization and globalization. Key Words: Globalization, Culture, Modernization, etc. (Abstract from: 10/30/2019 https://sites.google.com/site/drsushilseducare/clubs-activities/scholar-s-bow-/3-globalization-with-respect-to-its-impact-on-indian-cu…).

That said, the apathy among the modern families, the teens and adolescents lies within. Apathy is a state of indifference, or the suppression of emotions such as concern, excitement, motivation, or passion. An apathetic individual has an absence of interest in or concern about emotional, social, spiritual, philosophical, or physical life and the world. Does it have any relationship in the present context of dealing about negativity? It has.

Thus declares Manusmriti:

The teacher (acharya) is ten times more venerable than a sub-teacher (upadhyaya), the father a hundred times more than the teacher, but the mother a thousand times more than the father (2.145).

Marital or parental discord, if allowed to rule in the family, creates catastrophic effects of negativity, among the mother and father, the reflection of which directly causes psychological injuries to child and adolescent besides to the mother and the father. That creates cordiality disconnection within the parents spreading it to the children of whatever age they may be. This leads to constant anxiety, frustration, helplessness, hopelessness and depression. These characters having engulfed into the relationship and thoughts of the parents, expand and enlarge towards the children and make the children suppressing and distressing, the cause of birth of negativity in their mind. They carry it in their mind as they grow and whatever positivity existed in them converts into higher level of negativity. Its effect adds to the agony of prevailing discord of parents burdening them increasing negativity not only in their own relationship, also in their relationship with their children. It is a very severe blow in the healthy growth of the children because of formation of negativity which may drive them to hopelessness and depression.

The present day cases of hopelessness and depression include this category of teenaged and adolescents. Whom to blame? The parents to blame. They knowingly or unknowingly are the cause and effect of the unpleasant situation staring at them. It takes away the very purpose of life. How to reconcile and remedy for rebuilding the mutuality, trust, confidence, love, affection, oneness and sustainable relationship? It can be done. How? Adjustment and harmony are the foundation of life. Egoism is temporary and cannot be considered as irreconcilable. The parents need to start inching towards appreciation of each other's qualities and abilities bestowed by God for betterment and bring them closer and closer that enables recognizing the qualities and abilities of both capable of enhancing mutual understanding, appreciation and affection. This would happen when each one of them maintains silence, discard acrimony. The mind signals submissiveness in place of aggressiveness, that is, it starts quietening known as Quietitude. From Quietitude emerges the positivity which possesses access to the Spirit of Soul (Atman), All kinds of negativity that existed among the parents will dissolve itself, the beneficial effects of which touch the children and rejuvenate them with positivity and strengthen self-belief, courage and confidence to live against all oddities.

If this is not realized in time, it drives towards increasing strain and stress that ultimately decides whether to continue the relationship or break it up. This process prolongs ignoring the fact that there are children, wherever they are, whose fate hangs on the outcome of the relationship between their mother and father. There is legal protection to both, that is, divorce. Divorce may help mother and father to separate themselves but what happens to their children that sense fails to prevail upon even the children are standing before their eyes because obsession of divorce overtakes the reality of life. The divorce process is protracting and takes several years under the divorce law. In regard to children, they cannot divorce mother or father. If any answer to be given how they would live after the divorce of their parents, this is to be given morally and maritally by both together. That alone secures the children's' future. However, with respect to law, it all depends on the orders of the Hon'ble Court which looks into overall impact of the divorce and also the best interests of the child or children. This is as per law but not natural that the children want to live.

Research has found the most common reasons people give for their divorce are lack of commitment, too much arguing, infidelity, marrying too young, unrealistic expectations, lack of equality in the relationship, lack of preparation for marriage, and abuse. These causes give rise to heat up, tension, and acrimonious arguments. In a situation of this kind, one should cultivate listening rather than reacting. Listening is learning. Through learning, maturity of mind enhances capable to prevent avoidable arguments. Avoidance of arguments creates stillness and oneness. In the Conscience attached to the Atman (Soul), there live love (prema), kindness (daya), compassion (karuna) and forgiveness (kshama). There is also Conscious (awareness). Egoism blinds these godly qualities present in every body and Soul, ego is the person - himself or herself, the mind having no form of its own. What has been stated earlier could be achieved by inculcating the godly qualities referred to which is not impossible if one wants to make it possible. Let us now consider the essence of those godly qualities:

➢ "Love lives by giving and forgiving; self-lives by getting and forgetting. Love can never entertain the idea of revenge, for it sees all others as oneself. When the teeth hurt the tongue, do you seek vengeance against the wrongdoer? No, for they both belong to you and are integral parts of your body. So too, when someone insults you or inflicts pain, allow your wisdom to guide you." "Selfless love is the source of happiness, truth, peace, sacrifice, endurance and all the higher values of life. There is no security and safety without 'Prema', the absolute, unalloyed form of love. Love is the most fundamental moral value."...... (Ref: "Sathya Sai Speaks" – Vol. XVIII, Chapter-2). (When the inner sense of what is right or wrong in one's conduct or motives, impelling one toward right action (conscious): to follow the dictates of conscience. the complex of ethical and moral principles that controls or inhibits the actions or thoughts of an individual, lodges securely in mind, it becomes wisdom – added by author)

- "Kindness in words creates confidence. Kindness in thinking creates profoundness. Kindness in giving creates love." -- Lao Tzu
- "Compassion is defined as the emotional response when perceiving suffering and involves an authentic desire to help.
- Forgiveness frees us to live in the present. ... Forgiveness allows us to move on without anger or contempt or seeking revenge. 'To err is human; to forgive, divine.'

These God given qualities are endowed only in humans to live together, love together, be kind to each other, shower compassion on each other and forgive error as human error without any intent of revenge. These also equally apply to human relationship with other beings on earth. Marriage is the integration of these qualities. Selfishness leads to their misapplication or misuse against each other because it is selfishness that sprouts negativity in mind. Erase selfishness altogether and feel the joy that springs. Selfishness is the root of ego which once erased disappears itself. This is the sense and essence of relationship in the married life. Instead of running, having nurtured the discordant, around the lawyers and courts of law that aggravate the effects mentally, maritally and monetarily, accept the godly qualities with humbleness and full faith which narrow down the chasm and link the mind to Conscience, an integral part of Soul (Atman). This is permanent. Live up to this understanding rather undermining each other's natural Spirit of Life. This is the process for securing and safeguarding the positivity in mind. Knowingly unknowing these qualities are tossing around the life. All other efforts are like doing for the sake doing to achieve a result, unpredictable whether it would be for good or bad for future.

My Life experience shows people asking 'who is God', 'where is God', 'I don't believe in God', 'it is all for saying without any sense' and so on. These questions are also true for those who are asking them. What such people are speaking is the reflection of their imagination about God as non-existent. It is good to listen to such questions because they afford opportunity to listeners also to test how firm they stand knowing about God or are they shaken as a result of such questions believing uncertainty entering into the domain of doubts? Those who firmly believe in God attempt to explain as they understood God which may or may not be convincing. This brings a gap between those who deny belief in God and those who believe in God. Both who are for and against on existence of God fails to understand the very essence of source. This essence of source, in my understanding, is the Atman or Soul residing in both kinds of people.

Without there being Soul or Atman, they wouldn't have asked those questions or answered them. That is, it is the existence of Atman or Soul by virtue of which they are alive for asking or answering. If we deny this basic concept of God, both types of people would not have been a living body. They are living because there is Atman or Soul residing in them, not able to recognize because of their predominant perception in mind, ignorant or blinded to ask this very basis to them. Fact is that no living body whether human or of any other being on earth can move an inch without the existence of Atman or Soul, whether that Being is doing good or bad thing is one's own creation facilitated by the ego.

Also, in almost all religions, traditionally, the new born are named from out of the religious Faiths. In Hinduism various names of God and Saints and Sages are named. For example, Rama, Krishna, Ishwar, Mahadeva, Sita, Lakshmi, Parvathi, Sarswati, Padmavathi, and so on. Today, we are in a newer age of names given to the newly born which are drawn from slokas from Sri Vishnu Sahasranama or Sri Lakshmi Sahasranama and likewise from many other slokas available in other Holy Books. This practice prevails mainly among the Hindus. I believe, so also may be the case, in other religions. Assuming to be so, for those who question the existence of God whether in Form or Holy Script, need to start their enquiry from their name and its relationship with God or Holy Script or the saints and sages. These names have not come on earth of their own or from somewhere else. The parents see in them godliness and holiness. What is needed is to know oneself how such name is originated and what significance that name embodies. A simple enquiry leads one to the origin of the name and its significance. Because the names so given are the inspiration from the names of God or Holy Script or Sages or Saints. Search for Truth starts here.

Desire in human is immeasurable. It adds on driving the human to search and secure it. Because it is the Desire always demanding something of the taste it desires. Desire is a sense of longing or hoping for a person, object, or outcome. The same sense is expressed by emotions such as "craving". When a person desires something or someone, their sense of longing is excited by the enjoyment or the thought of the item or person, and they want to take actions to obtain their goal. Author considers himself as not competent enough to precisely describe, analyse, pinpoint the various aspects of 'desire', not being a qualified medical professional, an expert, spiritual master. Author considered appropriate to rely upon the Expert's views on the subject and, for that, reproduced below excerpts from an Article which could be said to contain every aspect of 'desire'.

Excerpts from the Article "The Problem of Desire - The psychology and philosophy of desire. Posted Nov 07, 2014 – authored by Neel Burton M.D., is a psychiatrist, philosopher and writer who lives and teaches in Oxford, England. Excerpts are reproduced herein for the benefit of the readers, presenting the vast and vivid account of the author on the subject matter:

"..........According to the Hindu Rig Veda (second millennium BC), the universe began, not with light, but with desire, 'the primal seed and germ of Spirit'.

Desires constantly arise in us, only to be replaced by other desires. Without this continuous stream of desires, there would no longer be any reason to do anything: life would grind to a halt, as it does for people who lose the ability to desire. An acute crisis of desire corresponds to boredom, and a chronic crisis to depression.

It is desire that moves us, and, in moving us, gives our life direction and meaning—perhaps not meaning in a cosmic sense, but meaning in the more restricted narrative sense. If you are at all reading this article, that is because, for whatever reason or reasons, you have formed a desire to read the article, and this desire motivates you to read it. ‘Motivation’, like 'emotion', derives from the Latin movere, ‘to move’. ....

The paradox of desire: We were born from desire, and cannot remember a time when we were without it. So habituated are we to desiring that we are not conscious of our desires, which only register if they are very intense or if they come into conflict with other desires. Meditation may not in itself prevent us from desiring, but it might give us a better insight into the nature of desire, which, in turn, can help us to disengage from unhelpful desires. ‘Freedom’, said the 20th century mystic and philosopher Krishnamurti ‘is not the act of decision but the act of perception.’

Try for just a moment to stem your stream of desires. This is the paradox of desire: that even the desire to stop desiring is in itself a desire. To get round this paradox, many eastern spiritual masters speak of the cessation of desire, or 'enlightenment', not as the culmination of an intentional process, but as a mere accident. Spiritual practice, they maintain, does not invariably or inevitably lead to the cessation of desire, but merely makes us more ‘accident-prone’.

The problem of desire: If desire is life, why should we desire to control desire? —For the simple reason that we desire to control life, or, at least, our life.

Hinduism may name desire as a life force, but it also calls it the ‘great symbol of sin’ and ‘destroyer of knowledge and self-realization’. Similarly, the second of the Four Noble

Truths of Buddhism states that the cause of all suffering is 'lust' in the broad sense of 'coveting' or 'craving'. The Old Testament opens with the cautionary tale of Adam and Eve: had these earliest of our ancestors not desired to eat from the forbidden tree, they would not have been banished from the Garden of Eden into our world of woe. In Christianity, four of the seven deadly sins (envy, gluttony, greed, and lust) directly involve desire, and the remaining three (pride, sloth, and wrath) involve it indirectly. Christian rituals such as prayer, fasting, and confession all aim, at least in part, at curbing desire, as does humility and self-abasement, conformity, communal living, and the promise of life-after-death.

All suffering can be framed in terms of desire. Unmet desire is in itself painful, but so is fear and anxiety, which can be understood in terms of desires about the future, and anger and sadness, which can be understood in terms of desires about the past. The mid-life crisis is nothing if not a crisis of desire, when a middle-aged person comes to the realization that his reality does not live up to his youthful, some might say immature, desires.

If desire is hurtful, so are its products. For instance, the accumulation of houses, cars, and other riches robs us our time and tranquillity, both in their acquiring and in their keeping—not to speak of their losing. Fame is at least as compromising and inconvenient as it is pleasurable, and can quickly turn into infamy. This need not mean that we should shun fame or riches, merely that we should not set out for them or invest ourselves in them. Greatness lies in living oneself with possessions stated before in a humble and mutually tied up understanding. This principle applies to all kinds of situations whether relationship between two or more humans or the family or the society or the nation, more in married life in particular because the new life comes on Mother Earth through those kinds of understandings as a result of consummation of the married life. I have already briefed up what is the marriage and its sacrosanctity. The desires that inter-mix or intervene in the married life that forces one or the other laid down limitations or boundaries among human beings; more so, among married ones drive one and all to towards destructive fate and future life. Let us understand this basic concept of Life given to the humans by God, live up to them through positive approach rather than negative questioning each other's desires or attitudes or actions one has to part and parcel of them."

While walking in the life journey, the distance in walking needs to be based on the principle of equidistance and if such distance shows more and more distancing, the distance gap widens which is crucial time in one's life to watch and come closer to each other to make Life journey to move tirelessly and smoothly lest when distance gap keeps further widening, each one will be moving in different directions in life that creates excessive edginess birthing the tragically unbearable situations, the shades of which start spreading in the married life journey including children's' hand in glove relationship, to which end it drives is not known either to the parents or to the children.

Life is to live incorporating togetherness irrespective to which category life belongs. One category that has more essentiality of this basis is the married life. Marriage itself is coming together after fulfilling the basic norms laid down under each Faith as have been stated before. The opposite of together is twitchy or tense all through one's life that separates itself from together. Sometimes, it may move towards walking marriage practised by some community in China.

Live-in-Partners: [Source: Live-in Relationship – Meaning, Benefits, Disadvantages, Rules and More - Updated on Oct 18, 2023

Wondering if a **live-in relationship** is the right choice for you?

"Well, though it sounds so glamorous, modern, and edgy… it comes with its own set of drama… yup! It's not drama-free just because of the missing legal affairs.

If you and your partner want to consider living together without getting married, this think-piece will highlight everything you need to know… before things get messy!

So, let's head right in…

Live in Relationship Meaning

In a live-in relationship, an unmarried couple commits to each other in a romantic relationship and decides to live together with physical, emotional, and even sexual commitment… but no legal commitment. The partners that choose to live together are called cohabiting or live-in partners.

Though cohabiting couples aren't legally married, they share domestic duties and responsibilities. In case they fall out of love, they move on without the legal drama of divorce.

There are several reasons people decide to live together instead of getting married. Some want to have the single status forever, some want to check compatibility before tying the knot. Others are just married already and can't marry another person legally… this is the usual case in polyandrous relationships.

If you're still uncertain about the difference between living together and marriage, keep reading…

Difference between Marriage and Live-in Relationship

Summary In marriage, your bond is socially and legally accepted and you get to enjoy all the benefits of marriage. But live-in relationships might be frowned upon, you're not legally accepted other than a particular nation, and you don't have spousal rights the same as marriage.

The chief difference between marriage and a live-in relationship is the legal status and its benefits. So, when you're legally married to your spouse, your bond is ritually, socially, and legally accepted. You and your spouse are legally bound to support and protect each other in the marriage.

In different nations throughout the world, various marriage laws and guidelines are formulated for a proper and healthy marital life. The laws even help spouses resolve disputes.

Especially, in diverse nations like India, marriage laws for every religion are different. Moreover, there are special laws for women's and children's protection and maintenance.

But when you're living with your partner, no law binds you both. Either of you can walk out on the other as you wish. Due to the lack of legality, there's no right to maintenance whether in the United States or in conservative nations like India.

However, the Domestic Violence Acts of most nations protect women against any violence in live-in relationships.

Wondering why don't people substitute marriage with a live-in relationship? Let's know in detail here…

Is a live-in relationship a substitute for marriage?

Summary Live-in relationships can never substitute marriages even though it seems so attractive due to the lack of legal rights and protection for each partner which later leads to insecurity.

In the modern age, marriage laws are more biased towards women to protect them from being exploited. However, not everyone uses them for defense… some take advantage of marriage laws and make their spouse's life miserable over the years.

For this, people want to be free from the twists and turns of law and enjoy a relationship without fear. On the other hand, some simply compare marriage with a form of unnecessary bondage that complicates life.

However, the commitment and will to continue a live-in relationship is much lower than that in marriages. So, ultimately, this type of relationship also grows miserable when couples start fighting.

Though a live-in relationship looks like a brighter and more glorious alternative to marriage, it's actually not.

But of course, live-in relationships come with their own set of pros. So, let's get to know them here...

Benefits of live-in relationship

Live-in relationships are a great way to know your partner and explore your connection. It's the perfect way to know if you're ready for marriage. You can also learn to deal with the responsibilities of marriage. So, let's take a closer look here...

1. The pain of goodbyes will be gone

In dating and relationships, you go on dates and then have to get back to your own homes.

In a cohabiting relationship, you won't have different destinations to return alone to. You won't feel lonely after a nice date and will spend more time even after getting home.

2. You can have each other right when you wake up

When you wake up in the morning, you can start your day together in live-in relationships.

On a busy weekday, you both can make breakfast together to pick up the pace... on peaceful weekends, you can take it easy, watch the sunrise, sip on coffee and chat together.

You share your most intimate and vulnerable moments together this way.

3. You can enjoy all kinds of couples' activities

Individuals living together also have ample time to spend together and enjoy small couple activities… which you either can't do if you live apart or need lots of planning to make it work.

For instance, you can't randomly bring your boyfriend/girlfriend over to cook together… you'd need to clean your space and prepare lots for that. Or, you can't surprise your partner with breakfast in bed or a massage on their stressful days.

4. Labels don't bog you down

Marriage comes with lots of pressure of expectations from family members. They want you to settle down, have babies and entertain each other's loved ones, and so on.

In live-in relationships, nobody is obliged to do all of that. You feel free and have peace of mind. You don't worry that "it's all because of that stupid piece of paper aka marriage certificate!" You stay together because you want to.

5. Ample space and privacy are on board

Since you're not obliged to do anything for each other's family members, you have ample freedom and personal space. You can be together as per your own rules and not get baffled by social pressure or expectations. You can grow together on your own terms.

6. You learn to handle finances together

In legally married couples that never lived together, managing finances out of the blue is a big shock. On the other hand, couples living together can take their time to understand how they can manage financial stress together.

Who pays which bill, how much you save, or how much you invest in necessities, you both learn the tricks bit by bit without being overwhelmed.

7. You can check for compatibility

Before you tie the knot, it's important to learn whether you guys are compatible emotionally, mentally, physically, and sexually. Without compatibility, a long-term relationship like marriage can't hold up.

So, if you start living together, you can test your compatibility with time. Even if you're not compatible in many terms, you can slowly compromise and meet in the middle.

8. It's easier to move on

If you find you and your live-in partner aren't compatible, you can simply break up and avoid serious issues of divorce and alimony. This is one of the biggest pros of living together over marriage.

In marriage, if you can't reach a middle ground even after trying, there'll be lots of issues other than divorce. A man will need to pay his ex-wife alimony until she gets married.

9. You get time to deepen the bond

While you spend more time living in relationships, you get enough time to learn more about each other at a deeper level. You get a long time to stabilize your bond and work through your differences. Even if things get tough, you might take a break and get back together.

Whereas in marriages, taking space away from each usually leads to divorce… and let's be honest, you won't consider each other romantically after the dirty court fight!

10. You'll be much more aware of marriage

Unmarried couples living together get a test drive of what marriage looks like. They won't be pressured to jump into this crazy institution called marriage out of the blue, get overwhelmed and smothered, and run for the hills.

You can decide whether you'll be able to stand a married life. And even if you decide to get married, you know exactly what to expect.

However, there are some issues with it, so let's check the cons…

Disadvantages of live-in relationship

Similar to how every relationship type isn't flawless, live-in relationships also have their fair share of problems. Yes, conservatives don't shun this type of relationship for NADA! ["NADA" is a Spanish term that has made its way into the English language, often used colloquially to mean "nothing" or "zero."]

So, let's know the real reasons here…

1. Breakups become tough

Individuals living together almost every moment of the day get emotionally entangled with each other. But sometimes, one partner feels that "this is my dream partner" while the other one decides to walk away. It takes a huge emotional toll on the one in love.

If you both shared the rent, you'll probably move out, and searching for a good place in that emotional condition is tough. But if you try to stay together until you find a space, your sweet memories will haunt you.

2. Infidelity might be a fatal blow

Since live-in relationships aren't legally secured, either partner might cheat on the other. This is a huge blow to the relationship, and to the loyal partner's trust and emotions. Due to the lack of legal binding, the cheating partner might refuse to take responsibility. Though cheating also happens in marriage, at least you can seek legal help for that.

3. It's not socially acceptable

Conservative societies and families don't recognize live-in relationships. Mostly, women get the shorter side of the stick. If anything goes wrong in the relationship, everyone blames the woman for being involved in the relationship instead of helping them. Your families most likely won't support you during fights… they might not even help you financially if you suffer.

4. Children born in live-in relationships feel insecure

Sexual relationships among live-in partners are pretty natural. So, unwanted pregnancy is also normal, to say the least. But if a woman chooses the wrong guy, he might demand her to get an abortion against her wishes or walk out on her.

Though some nations like India have laws to force the father to pay child support in live-in relationships, the child grows up with lots of difficulties, shame, and insecurity in the conservative society.

5. You're not legally protected

There are lots of benefits of marriage starting from income tax, to inheriting each other's property without putting each other in legal wills. You won't have any legal rights to see your partner if they fall seriously ill. If your live-in partner passes away before making a will, their family will claim their property and can legally deprive you.

Does that mean you can't have a live-in relationship? Of course, you can! But for that, let me tell you some…

Rules for Live-in Relationship

While live-in relationships are tricky to maintain and work with, it's not impossible. If you and your partner love each other enough, you will try to make things work. For a long-lasting relationship, first get these basics down to your fingertips…

1. Discuss money affairs

Since you both will run the household together, decide who will take care of which part of the finances before you move in. It's much better to clear any misunderstandings while your lives aren't tangled yet. Sit together and create a strategy so that nobody gets the shorter end of the stick. You both must be open and honest about your thoughts.

2. Allocate the chores responsibly

Whether it's getting groceries, cooking, cleaning, or even changing the car oil, distribute these responsibilities proportionally. Don't expect your partner to do everything or let your partner push it on you every time.

It'll be great if you can create a routine and stick it on your refrigerator or somewhere noticeable to reduce issues of forgetfulness. Equal chore distribution will also build a happy relationship.

3. Be clear about your intentions

Don't move in with a one-night stand or a weekend fling. Move in with someone you had a steady relationship for at least one year. Make sure you both want to stay together for a long time. Remember the highlight of living together is bond strengthening and not sexual satisfaction or an exciting adventure. If you move in with someone who only desires your body but doesn't want you for the long run, you might experience major emotional trauma.

4. Create plans for unwanted pregnancies

Whether you're a man or woman, don't bet on unwanted pregnancies. Use protection and take birth control together. Plan for unwanted pregnancies beforehand because protection is never 100% secure. Because being a woman you don't want to be left to fend for your child alone if your man leaves you… or, being a man, you don't want to fend for child support when you can't handle it.

5. Promise to deal with problems together

With time, you both will have lots of issues with each other. Make sure you don't forget that you're both on the same team. Don't fight each other… fight the problems together. Learn to communicate and resolve problems together. Take a deep breath before spilling bitter words and take space if you're too agitated. If needed, seek relationship experts for better ideas.

6. Don't turn away from sexual desires

Though unwanted pregnancies are scary, take your time to explore your sexual desires and fantasies. A good sexual connection can help you understand your sexual, physical, and even emotional compatibilities and whether the relationship can work in the long run. Even if the glimmer of hope is too small, you guys can still try!

7. Try to let each other have a life

While you live together, try to allow personal space and time for each other. If you always try to hog each other's free time, nothing good will come out of it. Instead, you'll be tired of each other and want to split sooner. Even when either of you faces troubles in your individual life, one mustn't meddle too much unless the other partner asks for help.

8. Never forget to save money

Discuss money-saving and investing methods together. Don't create joint accounts too fast. Keep control on your money but don't be shy about suggesting ways to save up. Moreover, if you have a bad breakup, your money will stand beside you… but if you have a joint account, you might get cheated big time.

9. Set boundaries and maintain them

Set boundaries about what each of you wants and doesn't under the roof and in your relationship. Perhaps, you don't want your partner to listen to music on speakers at 2 in the morning… or they want you to be more organized. Build dating boundaries… Can you guys date or flirt with other people? If your partner borrows money, when must they return it to you? Discuss the hard parts, write down your boundaries, and maintain them mindfully.

10. Learn to accept each other

You and your partner are meant to have different tastes in food, aesthetics, leisure activities and so much more. It's wonderful if you can appreciate each other for your differences. So, don't force each other to change your inner circle or likes. Accept each other wholeheartedly and broaden your horizons. Don't pretend to be someone you aren't and let your partner also accept you.

11. Own your mistakes

Perfection was never real… so, you guys will naturally make mistakes at some point. Remember to not become defensive… take a moment to think about your actions, how that wronged your partner, and how they feel. Once you understand your mistake, apologize from your heart with the reasons and tell them what you'll do to make up for it this time and prevent it from repeating. This will prove your commitment and things will eventually get better.

12. Set your priorities straight

Sometimes, you must prioritize yourself… Other times, you must sacrifice your happiness for your partner. There's no straight formula for this, so you must think carefully during these situations. Compare the pros and cons of both sides of the decision. This way you'll make better decisions and regret less. Otherwise, regrets can ruin your bond.

13. Don't take relationship advice from just anyone

Whenever you get into fights or have difficulty deciding something, you'll seek an outsider's help. But make sure you don't blindly trust anyone. Don't take others' words seriously unless they have your and your relationship is best in their mind. Choose to talk with another experienced live-in couple or seek relationship experts.

14. Think about getting serious

Whether you aim to get married soon or never wanna get married, sit and talk with your partner. You might never know… your partner might have their own opinions about marriage. If you talk about it before, you'll lower the chances of hurting each other with expectations. So, decide how long either of you can or wish to stay in live-in. Set a time when you guys wanna tie the knot.

15. Be prepared for the end

Even after everything, the relationship might not work out and you might split. You might get extremely invested in this relationship and be hurt if you break up. So, create a plan to heal yourself and move on instead of reliving past memories. Don't force your partner to stay back or be the crazy and toxic ex. For this, make sure you don't detach yourself from loved ones as you'll need them. However, before you jump into one, don't forget to check in with your local and national laws. Let's check a few here…

Legal Status of Live-in Relationship

Even if you love your partner a lot, you mustn't overlook the law ever. Otherwise, you might get penalized or sentenced for breaking the law or you might be at a disadvantage if anything goes wrong while living together. So, let's check a few here…

1. The United States of America

In the greater parts of the US, people are more accepting of cohabitation or live-in relationships. California allows live-in partners to get registered under the Domestic Partner Registry which helps them enjoy a few limited legal recognition and rights similar to marriage. As per US Cohabitation Agreements, cohabiting partners have the right to palimony, i.e., grant maintenance to the woman.

2. The United Kingdom

In the UK, live-in couples have no rights similar to that of married couples. They can't inherit properties unless they mention each other's names in a will. However, any child born from the relationship will be given equal care financially and emotionally by both parents as per their law.

3. France

In France, same-sex and opposite-sex couples sign *pacte civil de solidarite* or civil solidarity pacts. [Author adds: In English, this means: In France, a **civil solidarity pact** (French: *pacte civil de solidarité*), commonly known as a ***PACS*** (pronounced [paks]), is a contractual form of civil union between two adults for organising their joint life. It brings rights and responsibilities, but less so than marriage. The PACS was voted for by the French Parliament in October 1999……..[Wikipedia] This lets couples have a social union and enjoy their life similar to married couples. A live-in partner can revoke the agreement anytime they want with 3 months prior notice to the other.

4. Ireland

Both opposite-sex and same-sex live-in relationships are legal in Ireland. But their law grants the right to demand maintenance and property share when couples split to the financially dependent one. The public is against that part. That law comes into effect only if a couple stays together for 3 years or they have a baby and the partners are together for 2 years.

5. Scotland

As per Family Law Act, 2007 of Scotland, couples living together are recognized and authorized legally. But if the couple breaks up, the financially dependent one has the right to demand monetary help from the other.

6. Australia

As per the Australian Family Act, 1975, de facto relationships can be built between opposite-sex and same-sex partners… even if they have a legal spouse.

7. The Philippines

In the Philippines, the rights of live-in partners are governed by the co-ownership rule. It allows both partners to own their total wages, salaries, or properties in equal shares during the relationship. However, they won't get any legal benefits from marriage.

8. China

In China, live-in partners sign a relationship contract. If they have a baby, the child's status and succession rights are no less than children born from legal marriage.

9. India

In India, live-in relationships can be a domestic cohabitation can be of 5 forms: an adult unmarried man and an adult unmarried woman an adult unmarried man and an adult married woman (mutually entered) an adult unmarried woman and an adult married man (mutually entered)

Two same sex partners:an adult unmarried woman/man and an adult unmarried man/woman (entered unknowingly – punishable under IPC). Other than the last type, all other live-in relationships are legal in India. [[**Author's personal view: The Rules specified hereinabove are of suggestive nature and as a matter convenience for self-conviction. Except one State in our country, Rules for Live-in Relationship have not been laid down. The Central Government has not laid down so far any Rules in respect thereof. The suggested Rules are to be accepted or rejected by oneself. One affected by breach of unwritten Rules by law, cannot have any legal remedy.This is author's personal view]**

10. Mississippi, Michigan, North Carolina, North Dakota, Virginia, Florida

These US states have strong laws that oppose cohabitation or live-in relationships of couples of the opposite genders. But of course, same-sex couples might get themselves out of this loop if they identify as roommates or something similar. So, if live-in relationships are legal in your locality, let's get going and work more on your bond…

How to make your live-in relationship easier?

Living together isn't easy at all in reality. It's nothing like what they show in romance dramas and novels, so you may expect the worst. But when the worst happens, don't give up and look around for more ways to make your relationship beautiful. Here you go with some tips…

1. Stop taking each other for granted

Put more effort into the relationship, flirt, go on dates, complement each other, surprise them with gifts, help each other with your chores, pamper your partner with a massage, cook for them, and so on. You can do a lot of things to make your partner feel appreciated, so it's totally up to you how you want to do it. Cherish your partner with everything you have.

2. Remember there's no connection between gender and chores…

Cooking and cleaning aren't just for women… Fixing the car or driving isn't just a man's task. Make sure you don't expect a particular chore to be done by your partner just because of your chromosomes. On the other hand, your partner will make mistakes with the chores. Remind them with positive thoughts… little questions like "why didn't you still take the trash out?" sparks stupid fights. Instead say "honey, don't forget the trash!"

3. Always use protection

Men, don't get too adventurous and skip the protection. Don't give excuses like "I don't feel good with a condom… can't you pop a pill?" The pill will prevent unwanted pregnancy, but what about diseases? Moreover, do you know what the pill does to her hormones? She might even go barren for that. Women, stop accepting him without a condom, you know both pills and pregnancy will be extra stress now and in the long run.

4. Choose who you're comfy as visitors

You both have a life other than your relationship. You might want to bring over your friends and family at times. So, discuss whether you guys are uncomfortable with any of the other people. Don't bring in people that make your partner uncomfortable to your love nest and it'll definitely reduce lots of potential fights. Or, you can bring them in with each other's consent around hours when your partner is away.

5. Be clear about your relationship status and labels

Do you plan to move in because you're in love but your partner thinks it's to save bills? Before either of you assume anything, know each other's reason behind moving in and what each of you thinks about the relationship. Stay on the same page and don't hold unrealistic expectations. On the other hand, if your live-in relationship doesn't work out well, let's head in here…

How to end a live-in relationship?

Live-in relationships may not work out… so, be grateful that you didn't get married and undergo a divorce. Don't curse your luck but thank yourself for being brave enough to know the end sooner. But if you're concerned about how to end things, follow these…

1. Let it out with your trusted loved ones

Discuss the situation with your trusted ones and know their insight. If they can help you find a different perspective, you might save the relationship. It's better to seek someone who has a live-in relationship.

2. Take time for mental prep

Be kind and don't jump in with a pre-breakup conversation randomly. This will also allow them to mentally prepare themselves. Ask your partner to make time for some "important and serious conversation". They'll understand it's bad news and choose a time when they can process it all properly.

3. Be candid about your situation

Tell them what the issue is clearly and don't beat around the bush. Discuss if there's any way to change the current situation. Ask about your partner's point of view. What they feel about the issue and whether they're willing to change anything. Talking might help you find a better way to deal with the situation.

4. Be kind and genuine during the conversation

Never use ultimatums like "If you don't change, we'll break up". That'll only spike your partner's defensive side. Instead, use more I statement like "To me *insert the issue* is an important matter in a relationship. So, I might be unable to continue the

5. Don't keep any hard feelings

Most couples have dramatic breakups which lead to further troubles. But you don't need that! Despite how angry and heartbroken you are, don't take it on your partner. Your partner is also quite devastated, so don't say anything unnecessary. Of course, don't take any slanders from your partner either.

6. Allow yourself some space

If you continue to stay in the same house after this conversation, your partner might mistake your words for a joke. So, crash at your friends or family member's place. Take space until the bad news sinks in your partner. Let them process it so you can have a clean break.

7. Discuss the process

Once they understand you won't change your mind, decide how you guys split. Discuss splitting of property sharing, finance splitting, rental lease, and moving out. Let them have an equal say in this and make sure you don't force them to do anything against their wishes.

8. Define healthy boundaries until moving out

Your partner might try to patch up while you guys still share the same roof. Don't share the same bed and if you guys don't have two beds, alternately use the couch.

Avoid sex, spending time together, working together, or helping each other with chores. These might confuse you and the breakup might get delayed.

9. Seek your support group

Reach out to an online community or understanding friends to heal yourself. Go on a vacation and party with your friends. Socialize as much as you can with people that make you happy and practice self-care. This will help you move on and distract you from the heartbreak. Try to surround yourself with positive people and get busy for a good cause. Learn a new skill, get a degree, or simply aim for a better job.

10. Check in with yourself

Though you must distract yourself from the pain, make sure you're healing. Check in with your feelings every night and fill in a journal. If talking with your loved ones doesn't help, seek a mental health professional. Don't feel shy to let out your emotions. Trust the process and it'll get better.

A word from The Pleasant Relationship

It's hard to say whether live-in relationships are a good choice for you or not. However, keep the laws and your rights in mind. Remember to not jump into a live-in relationship unless you're truly sure and have no doubts. Don't get pressured into it… refusing to move in doesn't imply you don't love someone. But if someone forces you to move in even when you're uncomfortable, that's fishy! Don't forget that you're two individuals before you're each other's partners. So, be respectful and don't take disrespect.

Chase your happiness and try hard to thrive together… things will work out eventually! …….

An excess of desire is, of course, called greed. Because greed is insatiable, it prevents us from enjoying all that we already have, which, though it may seem like little, is far more than our forebears could ever have dreamt of. Another problem of greed is that it is all-consuming, reducing life in all its richness and complexity to nothing but an endless quest for more.

Desires in practice: That our desires are not truly ours is easy to demonstrate. When we make a New Year's resolution, we declare to ourselves and to others that, in some small measure, we are going to take control of our desires, implying that our desires are not normally under our control. The same goes for vows and promises. But even with the most solemn and public of marriage vows, we often fail to prevail.

Moreover, it is often over the least consequential desires, such as what to wear or what music to listen to, that we seem to exercise the most control, while whom we lust for/fall in love with seems mostly if not completely out of our control. Yet, a single rogue desire can lay waste to the best intelligence of half a lifetime.

In many cases, we simply don't know what we desire. But even when we do know what we want, we cannot know for sure that it will be good for us. A young man may dream of studying medicine at Oxford, but realizing his dream could mean that he is run-over by a bus three years hence, or that he never realizes his far greater potential as a novelist. Whenever our desires are frustrated, we ourselves should not feel frustrated, because we cannot be sure that what we wanted would truly have been good for us…………………

In closing: Luckily, there is no need to imitate Diogenes, and still less to banish desire. Instead, we need to master desire, because, paradoxically, it is only by mastering our desires that we can live life to its fullest. And it is only by mastering our desires that we might at last find some measure of peace."

Forgoing Article explains about the desire and, at the end stated "........we need to master desire, because, paradoxically, it is only by mastering our desires that we can live life to its fullest. And it is only by mastering our desires that we might at last find some measure of peace." What is mastering of desire? "The Mastering of Desire does not mean (as some suppose) the "killing out" of all Desire. In fact, as all careful students of the subject well know, it would be impossible to kill out all Desire, for the very act of "killing out" would be actually, itself, a response to a desire—a desire not to desire, as it were. Mastery of Desire really means the control, management, and direction of Desire by the Ego. The Ego may decide that a certain set of desires be repressed, or shut off, and prevented from expression in action or thought. Again, it may decide that certain desires be encouraged, cultivated, and stimulated, so that they may be able to exert a greater pressure and power in expression in thought and action. And, finally, it may decide to direct into a certain channel the force of a certain desire, so that some particular action may receive its concentrated and firmly directed power. In all of these cases, the Ego manifests Mastery of Desire." (Source: PSI TEK – Master of Mind – Mastery of Desire posted on website.)

Aristotle said - "I count him braver who overcomes his desires than him who conquers his enemies; for the hardest victory is over self."

According to James Allen, "Self-control is strength. Right thought is mastery. Calmness is power."

Above Quotes take us to the point which we dealt in earlier part and left behind. Factors that come out from these Quotes on mastering the Desires, control, management, and direction of Desire by the Ego, to overcome the Desires the hardest victory is over self and "Self-control is strength. Right thought is mastery. Calmness is power." What the Quotes have said is the Truth and right means to master the Desires. In the Quotes referred to, the elements emerging are control, management, direction, victory over self, Self-control, Right thought and Calmness. Those were to stop negativity and prod positivity in our thoughts to eliminate the evils flowing from the negativity and invite the loveliness of nature to live on from positivity. The negativity is unnatural while positivity is natural. One embarking upon negativity is like diving into the sea without the knowledge of nature of sea and experiencing unbearable pain from the environment prevailing in the sea. It is the inevitability of the negativity. If this is stopped, the positivity is born. The established process for attainment of such state of mind is the same as applicable for controlling the wilder and wandering mind until one is able to quieten it through self-practice and self-control upholding the supremacy of Quietitude. Quietitude is characterized by the same connotation of control, management, victory over self, self-control, right thought and calmness considered to be bedrock for the control of Desires. Desires have both negativity and positivity. The purpose of the process is to win positivity over negativity. This gives life real meaning of living on earth while negativity drives one to wilder part of the earth with chaotic conditions making the human being more akin to wildness in behavioural aspect of life.

Togetherness is not an independent element in itself. It incorporates in itself several other elements that form the sense of togetherness. What the author submitted so far on this subject is only the appearance of skin in the body without any flesh which if continued uncared may lead to darkening of the skin which means body is turning into impair leaving the strength that combines various elements in body; ultimately the body is bound to fall down of its own. This concept of togetherness calls for a close understanding of each element in the body that ensures the togetherness of the body. The author wishes to expand this concept to bring out what constitutes togetherness in a democracy and which factors contribute its withstanding against the whirlwind. Online Dictionary defines it as "Synonyms for together concertedly, conjointly, hand in glove (or hand and glove), jointly Words Related to together collectively, mutually, reciprocally, unanimously, unitedly cooperatively, symbiotically Phrases Synonymous with together in concert. Antonyms for together apart, independently, individually, separately, severally, single-handed. The consequential effects of the former meaning is its bedrock while that of the latter meaning is keep breaking within the body of democracy continuously on one or the other pretext. Important of all, what circumstances formed the basis for the evolution of the togetherness in the life of democracy.

INDIA was plundered by foreign invaders on many occasions in its history – more so after the Eleventh Century. India that was before invasions wore its originalistic look – a look that was characteristically Bharatiyata or Indianism outclassing in culture, morality, humanity and above all adorability. Such image comes before one's eye when one sees mythological and historical recaptures in mythological and historical writings, films and serials – a reminder for one to remember them through one's life. Beauty lies in their adaptation as far as possible individually and nationally as we pace up with progress underneath of which resides recognition of a most civilized era with full of human values and justice for all.

Then we entered era of freeing the country from foreign stronghold – the Freedom Struggle. This struggle span over more than fifty years from within and outside the country. Freedom Struggle evoked voice of oneness and embraced sacrifices of the people involved in various forms including their lives. Freedom was won. Then followed three major wars the country faced with its neighbours. These wars witnessed high morality, courage and conviction of the Indian Army and sacrifices the soldiers made for the sake of their country and for protection of future generation

National Pride is the positive effect that the public feels towards their country as a result of their national identity and self-developed economy. It is both the pride and sense of esteem that a person has for one's nation and the pride or self-esteem that a person derives from one's national identity. Patriotism is the zealous love for one's country. It's like a disease that every man carries. It spreads from one soul to the next like an unstoppable wildfire. There is no cure for such a disease; for this is one of pure determination and pride. (Google search). This is first part of National Pride. Its second part is the contentment of the country ethically, educationally, economically, confidence to deal with any blow and to stand as one amongst many and take the challenge of any kind in that spirit.

National Character and National Pride remained outside the domain of peoples' growth eroding and eating away the core strength of the Nation. Nations survive not by modern weaponry but by strong commitment, honesty, sincerity and gratefulness which form essence of National character and National Pride and a Nation without them is like holding in hand an empty barrel. Nationalism, National Character and National Pride conjoin people and make Nation free of corruption, dishonesty, insecurity, greed, selfishness, discrimination, communalism and anti-Nationalism. A Nation bereft of them is like building a castle on sand waiting to stumble. Let us remember that Nationalism, National Character and National Pride together form THE ULTIMATE STRENGTH AND GLORY OF THE NATION.

We voice collectively "BHARAT MATA KI JAI". Bharat is India and India is Bharat. Blood of every Indian is made of India or Bharat. This means that Indians are one and similar to a family of same blood. This should have guided us sentimentally and emotionally in our acts and deeds and our duty towards the Nation as it did during fighting for the freedom of the country. We continue to consider ourselves differently based on caste, creed, religion etc. in doing our duties whether in government, business, politics, educational systems etc. and do not shy of demanding graft from own brothers and sisters which amounts to self-cheating if not treachery. Those who indulge in corruption and in unlawful and illegal means to enrich themselves are at par with people whom we call dacoits with only difference that the methods followed are different, the former does it in a seemingly lawful and honorable way and the latter does it as part of profession liable for severe punishment which is not so in the former case where they find escape routes by searching someone else as a scapegoat.

Let us remember though languages we speak are many but we know we are all Indians; every faith in the country should flourish and all faiths together form National Faith. Like music is made melodious by combination of different musical instruments, the melodious voice of the nation is made by combination of different languages. Democracy should constantly strive for justice to every citizen and wrongdoing to none. Speaking and writing by public leaders in print and electronic media or otherwise based on castes, class and religion, even after seventy five years of independence, shows our democratic immaturity and audacity when we know well all of them form together to make One India and Peoples' Will, Saneness of eminent persons, Serenity of elected representatives and Sagacity of legal luminaries of the country that guide the Nation. LOVE ALL AND BE LOVED BY ALL. This is the culmination of the national jewels submitted hereunder, without which there can't be a sense of nationality and belongingness. Why I brought this subject which is out of context in this book? All that I have brought together as hereunder form the genesis of love and togetherness, the call of this book.

"The Indian National Flag represents the hopes and aspirations of the people of India. It is the symbol of our national pride. Over the last seven decades, several people including members of armed forces have ungrudgingly laid down their lives to keep the tricolour flying in its full glory. We find today many sections of people talking day in and day out about Nationalism, National Flag and Bharat Mata Ki Jai. Is it not self-insulting to talk about them which are inseparable from a Nation irrespective of incoming and outgoing ruling parties at the Centre and the States? We seem to have not understood their significance lying beneath every Indian's Conscience.

Are we to assume that those who had different faiths and proud of being Indians who lead this country before its Independence and after it became Republic lacked instinct to raise controversies on Nationalism, National Flag and Bharat Mata Ki Jai? Whereby, are we also to assume that we are more learned literally and ideologically than those Great Men and Women? Seventy five years after our Independence, we considered it necessary to enter into controversies over the National Integrals - Nationalism, National Flag and Bharat Mata Ki Jai? Why? Has it made any difference in our mental moment than those Great Men and Women lived. If so, describe the difference to justify. If not, why are we keen to spiral up something or the other hurting each other's sentiments and interests of the Nation? Is it not our core strength to stand together to forge ahead Nation's economic progress, prosperity and peace, the only way to liberate oneself from prejudices and strive to live with dignity and self-respect and not to stand apart with miseries of living and self-disrespect? Let us change and strive to maintain National Integrals free from political, social and religious choruses. Let us make them an integral part of our Consciousness and Conscience which together guide us in positive direction for strengthening our efforts to make the country strong to withstand any onslaughts and to accelerate the economic development that signals the arrival of the prosperity.

Human values are the principles, standards, convictions and beliefs that people adopt as their guidelines in daily activities. Principal human values are the foundation on which professional ethics are built. They are a set of consistent measures and behaviors that individuals choose to practice in the pursuit of doing what is right or what is expected of them by society. Most laws and legislation are shaped by human values. Human values are passed by parents to their offspring soon after childbirth and are instilled throughout the children's upbringing. As they grow, children learn more values from their peers, religious leaders, teachers, friends and society at large. These attributes include honesty, trustworthiness, diligence, discipline, fairness, love, peace, justice, care for one another and being mindful of the environment, including plants and animals.

News reports also state that some religious organization(s) asked people not to sing the national anthem at the particular place of learning during Independence Day (celebrations) and that the administrative authorities held the view that it would affect law and order situation and brotherhood that might even invite invoking penal provisions under the relevant law. One of the respected persons of a section stated to have said that the Indian Constitution has given the right to follow own religion and any action for not singing national anthem would be contested in a court of law. This is another side of expression of extreme emotion. It is to be acknowledged that freedom of religion would not have been available to any section of the people had India not attained its Independence and thereafter not adopted the Constitution that guarantees freedom of religion.

Independence Day thus acquires a character of independency to the exclusion of any other consideration including religion. This independency was attained with spontaneous collective efforts of all sections of society in India. Independence or Independence Day is independent of religion and calls for same collective echoing of voice that was echoed for attainment of Independence. National Anthem is an integral part of the Independence or Independence Day, one of the proud occasions for the nation that invites every citizen of the nation to celebrate and the celebration includes singing of National Anthem as per the provisions of The Prevention of Insults to National Honour Act, 1971 No. 69 of 1971 (23rd December, 1971) (Amended by the Prevention of Insults to National Honour (Amendment) Act, 2005) No. 51 of 2005 (20th December, 2005).

Is it anything to do with freedom of religion which is born out of the Independence and Republicanism? National occasions and interests stand above all other considerations of whatsoever nature and accord equal place to all the sections of the society as well as expects every section of the society to observe the same echoing sentiments as observed by the other sections of the society, as matter of expression of honor, respect, unity and solidarity. Doing anything contrary to this fundamental function of the each and every section of the society amounts to self- breach of trust the nation has placed in them.

There is no 'present' without the 'past' and there is no 'future' without the 'present'. Dusk of each day becomes past, the dawn of each day becomes present and the unknown next day becomes the future. The present always strives to look back to the past in every sphere of human life and endeavours to enhance itself over what existed in the past and looks to the future to help sustain such enhancement and enshrine. To continue to adjust with and improve the past is the process of the present, disregarding the past is like disapproving one's own genealogy and approving the past is the sign of one's reverence to and self-enrichment.

Great saints and writers undeniably acknowledge what existed in the past; what all happened in the past shown to the present in scriptures and writings moulded into pictures and films because that is based on the belief that people who lived then were witnesses whose evidence continues to be valid today. If not, generations to come will continue to ask the same question what we are asking today. When what is happening today, to which we stand as the living witnesses, becomes past tomorrow, generation born next day will say the same words what we are saying today 'where was the past and how one should believe there was past and so and so happened in that past'. None of the bygone generations could talk about the future, so also is the case with the present generation. Foundation of today is the one built by the past and what kind of structure one wants to build over that foundation - a more stronger or weaker structure – is the function of the present, resting on the future to hold on to it or destroy it, all depends upon the articulation and architecture the present chooses to apply for the aspirants of the next generation. Traditions can be said to consist of three Layers – First, Family Tradition, Second, Religious Tradition and Third, National Tradition. Each has its own age-old defined functional jurisdiction. Societies and the nations survived in the past on this primacy with all of them become bounden by the National Tradition. Attempts to redefine their functional jurisdictions would be disastrous leading to self-extinction. Soundness of mind and body of the societies that make the nation rests on this foundation.

One can notice that the relationships between castes are lately showing signs of reconciliation and relaxations. This view becomes more clearer when one sees around food sharing between castes and a lot more eating done at local restaurants, unification of minds and behavioural attitudes at all the public places such as hospitals, travel systems, festive occasions, functions, occupational pursuits, working environment, schools, colleges and professional institutions and organization. Many have now taken up newer occupations that do not relate to their caste, such as government jobs, teaching, retail and services. One can also see obscuring caste considerations in villages in terms of wealth, power land ownership. The thinking that purity and pollution is caused by the lower castes has diminished in the public. Education and awareness of equalization among the castes and women has already reached the shores in urban and rural areas of the country.

Word intolerance has become rather manifested in itself manifold meanings and misgivings. Bigwigs in the society and the learned and scholars in the academia print and electronic media as well as the people in the political realm are impatiently expressing and writing about the intensity of intolerance the country is said to be undergoing. An online dictionary defines word "intolerance" to mean, among other meanings, "lack of toleration; unwillingness or refusal to tolerate or respect contrary opinions or beliefs, persons of different races or backgrounds, etc." We are now clear about the meaning of intolerance in the context in which the word is occupying prominence presently.

Few questions before we proceed further. Where is it, how is it, why is it and who has made it so much irritable as to open up a wide debate? It is made mainly in relationships between the castes, creed and religions, wantonly, to provoke or to belittle and is made by a fanatic floating in once own ideological dream conscious of the fact that it is discriminatory and derogatory to the person against whom it is made. It is not realized that we are of the persons of the same nation, following our own faiths, working together, socializing together and above all defending the nation together. It is insulting today when a high profile person is appointed to higher post is referred in the print and electronic media as belonging a particular caste. It is high time that the government should consider to ban this usage and made punishable under the provisions of the relevant laws in force, the enforcement of which has so far been ignored. It is dangerous to the society and the nation to remain blind to such usage. It is shameful to do so. It is an insult not only to the person against whom it is made but to every citizen of the country as such utterance or gesture is an insult to nationality irrespective of to which caste, creed or religion such national belongs. This has become a handiwork of idling ideologists transgressing into other faiths in the society forgetting that the very faith which they are practicing prohibits making such utterances or gestures and impetrates to treat everyone first as human and then as a national but never as one belonging to one caste, creed or religion. This is the message of Holy Scriptures of all faiths to all humans and nationalists.

Change is the single most important feature of contemporary human experience when everything is moving in breath taking speed. The change which enthuses an enlightening sense that human should be more loving, compassionate, kind and caring not only to another but all other creatures on Mother Earth is a moving change, THE LIFE. Humankind must have a flowing, flexible, adapting, growing, innovative, creative consciousness, rather than a fixated, attached, constricted, stagnating consciousness. All religions, all prophetic utterances, all forms of worship and all kinds of rituals are like different streams join to make different rivers, ultimately merging into the ocean. An acquisitive, body focused mode of consciousness breeds conflict and sorrow whereas a sharing, self-focused mode of consciousness enjoys happiness, harmony and spontaneity. The ancient values as envisioned in all Holy Scriptures teach us the way of life in individuals, in society, in governing system and the people who lead the people as their leaders, ignorance of which will only lead to further humiliation and irretrievable downfall of humankind and hence the governing system in the country. This creates undercurrents not visible on the surface but has the potential to shock everyone like the one touching a leaking electric wire that drives towards serious injuries or even instant death.

An incident that happened recently where "Pakistan Zindabad' was voiced in the Legislative Assembly in one of the Southern States reported about the activities amounting to anti-national. There is law to take care of such situations. But, unfortunate part of it is that today's political parties with different ideologies consider such activities as not anti-national and hence no need to take note of them leave alone action in respect thereof. It was stated to have been said that such utterances are of pinching nature and not a crime under the relevant law of the country. Likewise incidents are also showing their ugly heads in other states every now and then. The comments, couching as part of freedom of speech, are bursting out not only with regard to anti-national acts or activities; also one's the Dharma followed by others in the country since the birth of the civilizations as moulded according to the preaching of the sagacious Holy Saints lived and made best ever efforts to sustain the Dharma. It is like poking one's nose into another either to show that his or her nose is longer than others or to self-shine in the media. Such person doesn't know let alone realize that his or her duty is to follow Dharma as per his or her own customs and practices to which he or she is bound but instead, forgetting this obligation, ventures to make nonsensical comments on others' Dharma of which he or she can be said as not knowing ABC of that Dharma. It is like say for the sake saying and keep the controversies cropping up as a matter of politically motivated habit.

".....Taken together, the motivational matching and the motivational distinctiveness analyses offer a clear conclusion. A message—whether it included credible information, moral value framing, or group norms—had a greater impact on beliefs and behavioural intentions when individuals' underlying motivations matched the nature of the message. This is particularly true relative to the no-motivation induction groups (i.e., motivational matching analyses), which is perhaps the most relevant comparison point given that virtually all prior work in this domain does not induce motivation in any way (i.e., employs a no-motivation/no-message control baseline). Indeed, as emphasized, the individual means when it comes to both beliefs and behavioural intentions consistently significantly exceed the baseline control. Thus, it may be that the aforementioned heterogeneity in prior work examining the effectiveness of different types of political messages stems from insufficient consideration of motivational dynamics……..” [Source: When and How Different Motives Can Drive Motivated Political Reasoning Robin Bayes Northwestern University James N. Druckman Northwestern University Avery Goods Northwestern University Daniel C. Molden Northwestern University - Political Psychology, Vol. 41, No. 5, 2020 doi: 10.1111/pops.12663]. The comments I adverted before are bottom down the human incitement and failure to respect the baseline order or dictum of political motivation which means the person making such comments is self-isolated not willing to know anything more than what he or she encaged within. Or to humiliate the people belonging to other Dharma which is meant for self-enjoyment at the cost of enjoyment of the other people.

THE GREATEST HUMILIATION IN LIFE IS TO WORK HARD ON SOMETHING FROM WHICH YOU EXPECT GREAT APPRECIATION, AND THEN FAIL TO GET IT. - E. W. HOWE

Should we say we have not undergone any change at all from the practices our ancestors followed for centuries in the past? That has not happened in any belief or Faith because the entire Earth environmental operation has been undergoing change from time immemorial. We have changed and continue to change that is the call of the hour we are living. The day we understand we are one among our different Faiths, one among our different cultures, one among our different languages, one among our different political and religiosity, we can say we understood what is 'oneness' which generates highest order of strength psychologically and physically to make us stand together to secure our own better living conditions as well as the interests of our country until our last drop of blood. That is what, I believe, every citizen wants to be which we could realize through our own conscience that leads us to a happiest moment of life for everyone regardless of the bickering by the political and religious leaders which works like breathing for their body, the latter is loaded with selfishness for power and money while the former unites us to protect each other's interests in every aspect of our and our nation's growth and welfare.

India is my country, your country and everyone's country who is its citizen. India is the family of Faiths; intertwined by their culture, mutual respect and living together for centuries though every century saw unfortunate and sad events that came and passed over; the Faiths continued to live as they lived in the past. The social integration has been the imprint and footprint of the living of the people. The people of each Faith stood as strong pillars against all odds and challenges the country faced now and then because of insatiable desire of its neighbors believing they are endowed with capacity to keep troubling the people next door. Every action has reaction and, if action is controlled, the reaction will disappear.

Poking in one's own affairs whether personal or official is always better than poking into others personal or official affairs, the former is the self-teacher and the latter is the lessons copied from others. Self-poking improves one's life and living while poking into others makes one to chase it; it comes back again and again to enjoy oneself by teasing others that eventually drives one to despair. So also the personal or political criticisms – constructive criticism builds one's stature, the stature of the society and contributes towards positive growth for the benefit of the people and the country. There is no substitute for positive growth.

The political or politicians' culture as existed when the country attained has and is undergoing sea change. The quality of political or politicians' system has undergone more towards degradation as comes out from the culture one could see in the present political system. Any culture bereft of decency and dignity is like dust storm blowing in the desert. The attitudinal level and degree of the politicians as being exhibited today is worst than even that of most illiterate person. Illiterate persons may not be educated but they cling to the dignity and decency in their interactions in the society. The language and words the politicians are using in debates and speeches are unworthy of that language and words because they are twisting and tuning them to the time but fail to understand that when silver is mixed with gold, it becomes more beauteous than mixing the iron with the gold. The language and words are like gold and silver and are to be accorded same dignity and decency as we accord for gold and silver. This is not there rather the politicians have learnt to mix iron with gold or silver which is creating an awkward scenario on the political platform that is reflecting the character of iron than gold or silver. The citizens know the difference but the politicians don't know what citizens know.

"THE WORLD WILL NOT BE DESTROYED BY THOSE WHO DO EVIL, BUT BY THOSE WHO WATCH THEM WITHOUT DOING ANYTHING" — ALBERT EINSTEIN

This is precisely what is happening in our country that we have learnt to swallow the dirty language and words without doing anything.

Idle devils always believe in creating and promoting devilish acts not knowing that other persons are not devils but human beings.

Next concern is why the cross religious bodies should not cross over and meet each other and together for the sake of welfare of the humanity and human beings rather boasting among themselves superiority over others. There is nothing known as superiority among the humans and, if there is one, it is only distinguishing oneself from the other selfishly. Every faith and every person within the faith is superior in himself or herself as equal human being. Let us remove the scars which are making each other's living miserable as they have been giving birth to negativity to mind growth driving towards hatred, crimes, militancy, terrorism all of which are overshadowing our own growth, development and lives. Let the great religious leaders meet together as often as possible to think and workout why we should not create an inter-religion institution to impart knowledge and learning to the people of each other's community and society to better appreciate the values and virtues embedded in each religious Holy Scriptures which will not only help develop a sense of brotherhood and sisterhood among ourselves but also go a long way to imbibe the values and virtues in developing each one of us within oneself which will spread fragrance of unified minds, love and togetherness – the essence of life.

Togetherness connotes and embodies permanent preservation of the life values and virtues handed down to us by our ancestors from the time of the birth of civilization on Mother earth and blood of the Freedom Fighters and the Army who fought for freedom to be enjoyed by the future generations which is achievable through the values of life stated before and a sense of INDIANNESS in every one of us that make us to LIVE TOGETHER AND ENJOY LIFE. Let us learn more about the values of life:

Excerpts from Speeches of Swami Vivekananda

(Source: Education for Character –Swami Vivekananda – Vivekananda Institute of Human Excellence, Ramakrishna Math, Hyderabad) (Eighteenth Edition- 2008)

EDUCATION: REAL EDUCATION IS THAT WHICH ENABLES ONE TO STAND ON ONE'S OWN LEGS. WE WANT THAT EDUCATION BY WHICH CHARACTER IS FORMED, STRENGTH OF MIND IS INCREASED, THE INTELLECT IS EXPANDED, AND BY WHICH ONE CAN STAND ON ONE'S FEET. BRING LIGHT TO THE POOR; AND BRING MORE LIGHT TO THE RICH, FOR THEY REQUIRE IT MORE THAN THE POOR. BRING LIGHT TO THE IGNORANT, AND MORE LIGHT TO THE EDUCATED, FOR THE VANITIES OF THE EDUCATION OF OUR TIME ARE TREMENDOUS.

STRENGTH OF CHARACTER: IGNORANCE IS THE MOTHER OF ALL THE EVIL AND ALL THE MISERY WE SEE. LET MEN HAVE LIGHT, LET THEM BE PURE AND SPIRITUALLY STRONG AND EDUCATED, THEN ALONE WILL MISERY CEASE IN THE WORLD. WE MAY CONVERT EVERY HOUSE IN THE COUNTRY INTO A CHARITY ASYLUM, WE MAY FILL THE LAND WITH HOSPITALS, BUT THE MISERY OF MAN WILL STILL CONTINUE TO EXIST UNTIL MAN'S AND WOMAN'S CHARACTER CHANGES. THE ROAD TO THE GOOD IS THE ROUGHEST AND STEEPEST IN THE UNIVERSE. IT IS A WONDER THAT SO MANY SUCCEED; NO WONDER THAT SO MANY FAIL. CHARACTER HAS TO BE ESTABLISHED THROUGH A THOUSAND STUMBLES.

SELF RESPONSIBILITY: MEN IN GENERAL LAY ALL THE BLAME OF LIFE ON THEIR FELLOW MEN OR, FAILING THAT, ON GOD, OR THEY CONJURE UP A

GHOST, AND SAY IT IS FATE. WHERE IS FATE, AND WHO IS FATE? WE REAP WHAT WE SOW. WE ARE THE MAKERS OF THE OUR OWN FATE. NONE ELSE HAS THE BLAME, NONE HAS THE PRAISE. THIS MISERY THAT I AM SUFFERING IS OF MY OWN DOING, AND THAT VERY THING PROVES THAT IT WILL HAVE TO BE UNDONE BY ME ALONE. THAT WHICH I CREATED, I CAN DEMOLISH; THAT WHICH IS CREATED BY SOMEONE ELSE, I SHALL NEVER BE ABLE TO DESTROY. THEREFORE, STAND UP, BE BOLD, BE STRONG. TAKE THE WHOLE RESPONSIBILITY ON YOUR OWN SHOULDERS, AND KNOW THAT YOU ARE THE CREATOR OF YOUR OWN DESTINY. WE MAY GO ON ACCUMULATING THINGS FOR OUR PHYSICAL ENJOYMENT, BUT ONLY WHAT WE EARN IS REALLY OURS.

POSITIVE THINKING: IN LANGUAGE AND LITERATURE, IN POETRY AND THE ARTS, IN EVERYTHING WE MUST POINT OUT NOT THE MISTAKES THAT PEOPLE ARE MAKING IN THEIR THOUGHTS AND ACTIONS, BUT THE WAY IN WHICH THEY WILL GRADUALLY BE ABLE TO DO THESE THINGS BETTER. POINTING OUT MISTAKES WOUNDS A MAN'S FEELING. MEN ARE TAUGHT FROM CHILDHOOD THAT THEY ARE WEAK AND SINNERS. TEACH THEM THAT THEY ARE ALL GLORIOUS CHILDREN OF IMMORTALITY, EVEN THOSE WHO ARE THE WEAKEST IN MANIFESTATION. LET POSITIVE, STRONG, HELPFUL THOUGHT ENTER INTO THEIR BRAINS FROM VERY CHILDHOOD.

CONTROL OF MIND: SELF BECOMES A FOOL AND LOSES INDEPENDENCE. SO, BY NON-ATTACHMENT, YOU OVERCOME AND DENY THE POWER OF ANYTHING TO ACT UPON YOU. IT IS VERY EASY TO SAY THAT

NOTHING HAS THE RIGHT TO ACT UPON YOU UNTIL YOU ALLOW IT TO DO SO; BUT WHAT IS THE TRUE SIGN OF THE MAN WHO REALLY DOES NOT ALLOW ANYTHING TO WORK UPON HIM WHO NEITHER HAPPY OR UNHAPPY WHEN ACTED UPON BY THE EXTERNAL WORLD? THE SIGN IS THAT GOOD OR ILL FORTUNE CAUSES NO CHANGE IN HIS MIND; IN ALL CONDITIONS HE CONTINUES TO REMAIN THE SAME. THE MAN WHO HAS CONTROL OVER HIS OWN MIND ASSUREDLY WILL HAVE CONTROL OVER EVERY OTHER MIND. THAT IS WHY PURITY AND MORALITY HAVE BEEN ALWAYS THE OBJECT OF RELIGION; A PURE, MORAL MAN HAS CONTROL OF HIMSELF.. HE WHO KNOWS AND CONTROLS HIS OWN MIND KNOWS THE SECRET OF EVERY MIND AND HAS POWER OVER EVERY MIND.

POWER OF THOUGHT: WE ARE WHAT OUR THOUGHTS HAVE MADE US; SO TAKE CARE OF WHAT YOU THINK. WORDS ARE SECONDARY. THOUGHTS LIVE, THEY TRAVEL FAR. EACH THOUGHT WE THINK IS TINGED WITH OUR OWN CHARACTER, SO THAT FOR THE PURE AND HOLY MAN EVEN HIS JESTS OR ABUSE WILL HAVE THE TWIST OF HIS OWN LOVE AND PURITY AND DO GOOD. EACH THOUGHT IS A LITTLE HAMMER BLOW ON THE LUMP OF IRON WHICH OUR BODIES ARE, MANUFACTURING OUT OF IT WHAT WANT IT TO BE. THE WORD AND THOUGHT ARE INSEPARABLE. THE EXTERNAL PART OF ONE AND THE SAME THING IS WHAT WE CALL WORD, AND THE INTERNAL PART IS WHAT WE CALL THOUGHT. EVERY THOUGHT PROJECTED FROM EVERY BRAIN GOES ON PULSATING, AS IT WERE, UNTIL IT MEETS A FIT OBJECT THAT WILL RECEIVE IT. LIBERTY OF THOUGHT AND ACTION IS THE ONLY CONDITION OF LIFE, OF GROWTH AND WELLBEING. WHERE IT DOES NOT EXIST, THE MAN THE RACE, THE NATION MUST GO DOWN. LITTLE

MANIFESTATIONS OF ENERGY THROUGH THE MUSCLES ARE CALLED WORK. BUT WHERE THERE IS NO THOUGHT, THERE WILL BE NO WORK. FILL THE BRAIN, THEREFORE, WITH HIGH THOUGHTS, HIGHEST IDEALS, PLACE THEM DAY AND NIGHT BEFORE YOU, AND OUT OF THAT WILL COME GREAT WORK. TALK NOT ABOUT IMPURITY, BUT SAY THAT WE ARE PURE.

SELF CONFIDENCE: THE IDEAL OF FAITH IN OURSELVES IS OF THE GREATEST HELP TO US. WHAT MAKES THE DIFFERENCE BETWEEN MAN AND MAN IS THE DIFFERENCE IS THIS SHRADDHA AND NOTHING ELSE. WHAT MAKES ONE MAN GREAT AND ANOTHER WEAK AND LOW IS THIS SHRADDHA. YOU HAVE IN YOU A THOUSAND TIMES MORE THAN IS IN ALL THE BOOKS. NEVER LOSE FAITH IN YOURSELF; YOU CAN DO ANYTHING IN THIS UNIVERSE. NEVER WEAKEN, ALL POWER IS YOURS.

STRENGTH OF LIFE: MY CHILD, WHAT I WANT IS MUSCLES OF IRON AND NERVES OF STEEL, INSIDE WHICH DWELLS A MIND OF THE SAME MATERIAL AS THAT OF WHICH THE THUNDERBOLT IS MADE. STRENGTH IS LIFE, WEAKNESS IS DEATH. STRENGTH IS FELICITY, LIFE ETERNAL, IMMORTAL; WEAKNESS IS CONSTANT STRAIN AND MISERY; WEAKNESS IS DEATH. THE REMEDY FOR WEAKNESS IS NOT BROODING OVER WEAKNESS, BUT THINKING OF STRENGTH. TEACH MEN OF THE STRENGTH THAT IS ALREADY WITHIN THEM.

POWER OF CONCENTRATION: TO TAKE UP ONE IDEA, MAKE THAT ONE IDEA YOUR LIFE; THINK OF IT, DREAM OF IT, LIVE ON THAT IDEA. LET THE BRAIN, MUSCLES, NERVES, EVERY PART OF YOUR BODY, BE FULL OF THAT IDEA, AND JUST LEAVE EVERY OTHER IDEA ALONE. THIS IS THE WAY TO SUCCESS, AND THIS

IS THE WAY GREAT SPIRITUAL GIANTS ARE PRODUCED. OTHERS ARE MERE TALKING MACHINES.

SECRET OF WORK: THIS LIFE IS SHORT, THE VANITIES OF WORLD ARE TRANSIENT, BUT THEY ALONE LIVE WHO LIVE FOR OTHERS, THE REST ARE MORE DEAD THAN ALIVE. BLESSED ARE THEY WHOSE BODIES GET DESTROYED IN THE SERVICE OF OTHERS. HIM I CALL A MAHATMAN (GREAT SOUL) WHOSE HEART BLEEDS FOR THE POOR; OTHERWISE HE IS A DURATMAN (WICKED SOUL). INACTIVITY SHOULD BE AVOIDED BY ALL MEANS. ACTIVITY ALWAYS MEANS RESISTANCE. RESIST ALL EVILS MENTAL AND PHYSICAL; AND WHEN YOU HAVE SUCCEEDED IN RESISTING, THEN WILL CALMNESS COME. IT IS LTHE LEVEL-HEADED MAN THE CALM MAN OF GOOD JUDGMENT AND COOL NERVES, OF GREAT SYMPATHY AND LOVE, WHO DOES GOOD WORK AND SO DOES GOOD TO HIMSELF. BY MEANS OF THE CONSTANT EFFORT TO DO GOOD TO OTHERS WHO ARE TRYING TO FORGET OURSELVES; THIS FORGETFULNESS OF SELF IS THE ONE GREAT LESSON WE HAVE TO LEARN IN LIFE.

UNIVERSAL RELIGION: MY CHILDREN, THE SECRET OF RELIGION LIES NOT IN THEORIES BUT IN PRACTICE. TO BE GOOD AND TO DO GOOD – THAT IS THE WHOLE OF RELIGION. I DO NOT BELIEVE IN A GOD OR RELIGION WHICH CANNOT WIPE THE WIDOW'S TEARS OR BRINGS A PIECE OF BREAD TO THE ORPHAN'S MOUTH.

IDEAL OF WOMANHOOD: IF YOU DO NOT RAISE THE WOMEN, WHO ARE THE LIVING EMBODIMENT OF THE DIVINE MOTHER, DON'T THINK YOU HAVE ANY OTHER WAY TO RISE. THAT COUNTRY AND THAT NATION WHICH DO NOT RESPECT WOMEN HAVE NEVER BECOME GREAT, NOR WILL EVER BE IN FUTURE. GODS

BLESS THOSE FAMILIES WHERE WOMEN ARE HAPPY AND WELL TREATED. DAUGHTERS SHOULD BE SUPPORTED AND EDUCATED WITH AS MUCH CARE AND ATTENTION AS THE SONS. THERE IS NO CHANCE FOR THE WELFARE OF THE WORLD UNLESS THE CONDITION OF WOMEN IS IMPROVED. IT IS NOT POSSIBLE FOR A BIRD TO FLY ON ONLY ONE WING.

Why BR Ambedkar's three warnings in his last Speech to the Constituent Assembly resonate even today

On November 25, 1949, he spoke of the need to give up the grammar of anarchy, to avoid hero-worship, and to work towards a social – not just a political – democracy. [Excerpts]:

Three warnings

If we wish to maintain democracy not merely in form, but also in fact, what must we do?

The first thing in my judgement we must do is to ***hold fast to constitutional methods of achieving our social and economic objectives***. It means we must abandon the bloody methods of revolution. It means that we must abandon the method of civil disobedience, non-cooperation and Satyagraha. When there was no way left for constitutional methods for achieving economic and social objectives, there was a great deal of justification for unconstitutional methods. But where constitutional methods are open, there can be no justification for these unconstitutional methods. These methods are nothing but the ***Grammar of Anarchy*** and the sooner they are abandoned, the better for us.

The second thing we must do is to observe the caution which John Stuart Mill has given to all who are interested in the maintenance of democracy, namely, ***not "to lay their liberties at the feet of even a great man, or to trust him with power which enable him to subvert their institutions"***. There is nothing wrong in being grateful to great men who have rendered life-long services to the country. But there are limits to gratefulness. As has been well said by the Irish Patriot Daniel O'Connel, no man can be grateful at the cost of his honour, no woman can be grateful at the cost of her chastity and no nation can be grateful at the cost of its liberty. This caution is far more necessary in the case of India than in the case of any other country. For in India, Bhakti or what may be called the path of devotion or hero-worship, plays a part in its politics unequalled in magnitude by the part it plays in the politics of any other country in the world. Bhakti in religion may be a road to the salvation of the soul. But **in politics, Bhakti or hero-worship is a sure road to degradation and to eventual dictatorship.** ……… [Emphasis added by the author]

What does fraternity mean? Fraternity means a sense of common brotherhood of all Indians – of Indians being one people. It is the principle which gives unity and solidarity to social life………..

The third thing we must do is not to be content with mere political democracy. We must make our political democracy a social democracy as well. Political democracy cannot last unless there lies at the base of it social democracy.

Eve of every national election witnesses political leaders standing heavily garlanded at highly decorated platforms delivering speech that echoes all around promising what they would do in the next five years if they were elected; they assure the people present of doing everything for their betterment with high priority for development, ending of poverty and terrorism and so many such other matters to attract moving minds of the people. They don't realize they had made similar speeches in the past elections; whether it would be good for them to repeat the same; they do it as they know memory of people is short. The speeches of the politicians landed us in 'fool's paradise'. Politicians have become more personalized that is severely shaking up institutional autonomy, a visible sign of degradation of democratic foundation. This is how the poverty, terrorism, loss of faith in secularism, due respect to past great leaders and lack of sense of mutuality, the essential spirit for economic development and security have increased in width and length causing anxiety and anguish to the people. Time we realized the Reality and are guided by the Reality

One may ask what relationship of what is stated before has with the title of this book.

My submission is that Togetherness is a Big Tree with hundreds of branches, each branch holding its own strength that makes the Big Tree not to worry about its weakness as long as its branches are strong. So also, Togetherness is a Big Tree called India that has different faiths, languages and cultures which are its branches. India also connotes the combination of these branches. As the Big Tree thinks it need not to worry about its weakness as long as its branches are strong, so also India needs to be assured by its branches to think that it need not to worry about weaknesses as its branches stated before are strong that ensure the understanding and unity of the strength achievable through the strength of the branches India is bestowed with. The combination of branches is Togetherness for India. India can be said to be together if the families, societies and citizens residing therein have a sense of belongingness of Indianness among them that builds a strong foundation to grow limitlessly for the benefit of the generations to come.

Let me now deal the breakdown of the marriages. I have already stated before the purpose of marriage and pros and cons of Live-in-Partner. As to the latter one, I consider hardly any need to enlarge it as one of the learned Writers has given the detailed account of that in the Article also reproduced before. That is self-contained and self-assessable by the interested persons or the groups. It is my duty to respectfully endorse what the learned Writer has accounted with regard to that subject. But, as an elderly person of 87 years, I also consider, to the best of my understanding, the doors that stand open for such relationship. Think twice, if necessary, more than twice and avoid hurriedness that may cost one entering into such arrangement dearly entangling the entire family and relations. Live-in-Partner concept presupposes no need to consult anyone including the family and relations that hides potential dangers with possibility of self-ruining the life. God has given liberty of life for everyone but such liberty that comes once in one's life has to be used such that liberty itself should not ruin one's life. I have also stated before through a Quote about what is the True Love. I repeat the same below for the convenience of the readers:

The Purity of Love is thus explained:

"WHEN OVER THE YEARS SOMEONE HAS SEEN YOU AT YOUR WORST, AND KNOWS YOU WITH ALL YOUR STRENGTHS AND FLAWS, YET COMMITS HIM- OR HERSELF TO YOU WHOLLY, IT IS A CONSUMMATE EXPERIENCE. TO BE LOVED BUT NOT KNOWN IS COMFORTING BUT SUPERFICIAL. TO BE KNOWN AND NOT LOVED IS OUR GREATEST FEAR. BUT TO BE FULLY KNOWN AND TRULY LOVED IS, WELL, A LOT LIKE BEING LOVED BY GOD. IT IS WHAT WE NEED MORE THAN ANYTHING. IT LIBERATES US FROM PRETENSE, HUMBLES US OUT OF OUR SELF-RIGHTEOUSNESS, AND FORTIFIES US FOR ANY DIFFICULTY LIFE CAN THROW AT US." - TIM KELLER – AUTHOR - THE MEANING OF MARRIAGE

Remember to apply the test of purity of love laid in the above Quote and then think and move forward. **It is also said that 'what have you done if you have ruined the chastity of the woman or if you have burnt the lamp during the day and want to live in darkness in the night.**

The idiom "marriages are made in heaven" means that the fate or destiny of who we marry is decided by a higher power, such as God, and not by human choice or action. It is often used to express the belief that marriage is a sacred and divine institution and that married couples have a special bond that transcends earthly matters.[Source: Marriages Are Made In Heaven: Definition, Meaning, and Origin - U.S.Dictionary Webpage]

If the marriages made according to the customs such as the one stated above are amenable to breakdown, it is not surprising that other kinds of marriages are more prone to the breakdown. Why one marries has been explained at length before and if this essence as brought out therein is of any concern to the married couple, all that is injected in between the couples driving them to the point of breakdown assumes a contrary character of the couple thought of before the marriage which happens not mainly because of lack of love or claiming superiority over the other or differences on certain matters but because of ceaselessly cultivating the grimness of the Ego which, if allowed to grow beyond one's control is bound to explode and enwrap the peaceful environment otherwise existed shattering and vitiating one that breeds the poison into one's body and spreads like cancer endangering the very marriage and life, more so of the growing children born to such couple.

There are hundreds of books and thousands of articles published about the marriage breaks and continue to be so even today. If one reads them, one get so much confused as to which way to follow because the intellectual person who writes such books or articles has one angle as to how to induce those people affected by such breaks in one's life opening various kinds of ways and means on how to make up the broken marriages or causes and remedies for such marriages and the line of treatment that could be helpful to become beware of them before and particularly after the marriage. It is good to read them as often as necessary for; such writings are based on lot of research and, may be, one's own experience. Such food of knowledge remains at all the times as supplementary food because the primary source of food lies within oneself. These are anticipatable by the intended couple either before the marriage or in the initial stages soon after the marriage. Based on such anticipation, signs of happier life or symptoms of strains start showing up. This is the critical time in one's life to go into depth within.

Every human has reasoning and logic but when these are overshadowed by ego, both the reasoning and logic become blind to the eyes. A person who develops such kind of gestures stands in a state of fixation. Let me explain what is reasoning and logic:

Reasoning and Logic?

In Hinduism:

'The category of reason is used in Hindu spiritual and philosophy in different senses. One can discern two broad usages: one, as a faculty of the mind that is, as an instrument of philosophical reflection and, two, as logic, that is, an instrument of argumentation. There is no exact Sanskrit synonym for the word "reason." The term buddhi is often used to denote reason as a faculty of the mind, and words like manana and vicāra are used to denote the act of reflection or contemplation. Anumāna is inference; it is one of the six pramāṇas or valid means of knowledge and is accepted by all the six schools of Hindu philosophy (darśana). The word Nyāya, after which is named one of the six schools of Hindu philosophy, means logic. Tarka and yukti are also words used to denote logic. These different words are used to denote different dimensions of reason.

In Islam

Verily, in the creation of the heavens and earth, and the alternation of the night and the day, and the ships which sail through the sea with benefits for people, and what Allah has sent down from the heavens of rain, giving life thereby to the earth after its lifelessness and dispersing therein every creature, and in His directing of the winds and the clouds controlled between the heaven and the earth are signs for a people who use reason. Surat al-Baqarah 2:164

In Christianity

Paul commands us to think about what he says. Use your mind. Engage your reasoning powers when you hear the word of God. Jesus warned what happens if we don't and what blessing may come if we do. In the parable of the soils, he said concerning the seed sown on the path: "When anyone hears the word of the kingdom and does not understand it, the evil one comes and snatches away what has been sown in his heart." Understanding with the mind is not optional. Our lives hang on it. And concerning the seed sown on good soil, he says, "This is the one who hears the word and understands it. He indeed bears fruit and yields, in one case a hundredfold, in another sixty, and in another thirty" (Matthew 13:23).

"BUT LIKE INFECTION IS THE PETTY THOUGHT: IT CREEPS AND HIDES, AND WANTS TO BE NOWHERE--UNTIL THE WHOLE BODY IS DECAYED AND WITHERED BY THE PETTY INFECTION... THUS SPOKE ZARATHUSTRA." — FRIEDRICH NIETZSCHE

I believe the readers will appreciate the meaning of reasoning and logic. Even then, as the above Quote cautions that a petty infection may cause such effects in the human body that mesmerizes the human until the infection shows its signs of growth in the body whereby the human mind starts decaying. In other words, the petty infection that is responsible for decaying the mind is Ego that has neither form nor colour but represents the human himself or herself. The reasoning and logic are the self – possessed weapons to prevent any signs of birth of the petty infection leading to decaying the body, more so, the mind. The mind remains in a state of utter confusion as to how to go about the signs of the petty infection. This is so because the mind doesn't have any form as stated before and is guided by the two controlling and overruling factors – one is positivity and the other is negativity. Online Dictionary defines 'positivity' as 'Positivity is the practice or tendency to be positive or optimistic in life. When we are positive, we engage in positive thinking, have positive emotions, and engage in positive behaviors like kindness and generosity. All of this positivity contributes to positive outcomes like improved well-being. Same dictionary defines 'negativity' as 'Negativity is a tendency to be downbeat, disagreeable, and skeptical. It's a pessimistic attitude that always expects the worst. Someone full of negativity is hard to cheer up, and they always expect the worst. Those who practice the Qualities, Justice and Equality in their life are able to cut the negativity at the root. This also is as understood by the author, having had the opportunity to know what the saints and sages said.

Once again I wish to convey as a matter of sense of necessity to the readers that the Godly Qualities that HE has attached with the human would greatly facilitate doing away with 'negativity', the source of miseries in life and in establishing 'positivity' in oneself that beckons Godly Qualities and makes the practitioner of these Qualities. There is always a Way Out in Life even in negativity once the positivity is lighted; the darkness of negativity disappears itself. It is my ardent desire and earnest hope that the young, the middle and the older people wake up to the call to live life as worth living along with beauteous Nature on Mother Earth. Rise above the negativity. Negativity is artificial made up of circumstances. Circumstances are moving clouds; one can also see Sun rays between the clouds – the HOPE that guides you to reality of life. Hold it strongly in your hand, the beckoning light to live cheerfully.

Swami Vivekananda observed that it is the focus the object attracts rather than the object itself. Example, when one is going on foot path or by cycle or by car or by bus or by train etc., one encounters many kinds of the objects in various forms, having beautification and attraction, naturally diverting one's attention. So also it happens in many other circumstances say, at work place, home, schools, colleges, sports, married life and so on. Their weight is felt in every one coming under those circumstances in life. Some see and pass through the object without feeling any attachment. Some others get attached. If someone gets attached to the object, the object settles itself in the eyes shifting it to thoughts (conscious) which passes it on to mind. Mind starts intensively dwelling on that object how to possess it disturbing the normal balance of thinking power and body. Once that happens, it rotates and repeats constantly creating vibrations of abnormality shaping up in the person. Its continued persistence roots negativity and, when that negativity assumes increasing intensity, it lays more and more focus on the object. Mind so set wanting somehow reach to the object making itself a hard process not knowing whether it would succeed or fail. This process causes negativity and mental torture which, if not timely ignored as just as an object seen in the ordinary course of life, leads to psycho-physical attacks in the person.

QUESTIONS YOU NEED TO ASK TO IMPROVE YOUR MARRIAGE

Questions to Know How You Can Improve as a Spouse

"First and foremost, it is important to acknowledge that you are doing your best as a partner. However, there will be points in your marriage where there are certain aspects that need to be altered, modified, or improved to ensure a strong and healthy relationship. Listed below are 30 questions that will help you determine the specific aspects of your marriage that need to be worked on.

1. Is there anything you wish that I would do differently as your partner?
2. Is there anything you wish that I would do differently as a parent?
3. Do you think I show you how much I love you enough?
4. What is your love language?
5. What are some things I can do to better show you my love?
6. Is our parenting system still healthy and effective?
7. Do you want to renegotiate or revaluate the way we distribute responsibilities?

8. Have I recently done anything to hurt your feelings?
9. How can I help you cope better with challenges that come our way?
10. Do you think I rely on you too much?
11. Is there something I do that you wish I would do more?
12. What is your way of showing me your love that I perhaps do not realize?
13. What needs does our marriage have that need to be better handled?
14. Do you feel as if our emotional connection has diminished over the years?
15. Do you think our intimacy needs to be worked on?
16. Is there something you need my help with right now?
17. What are the strengths and weaknesses that I bring to our marriage?
18. Do you think we spend too little, just enough, or too much time together?
19. What can we do to improve as a team?
20. On a scale of 1 to 10, how would you rate me as a partner and as a parent? What would help my current score improve?
21. How has our marriage changed over the past few years?
22. Do you think our marriage has changed for the better or worse?
23. Do you feel safe talking to me about uncomfortable topics?
24. How do I make you feel more comfortable talking about serious topics?

25. Am I supportive or encouraging enough in your endeavours?
26. Is there anything you wish that I would ask you more frequently?
27. Do I make you feel respected, honored, and appreciated?
28. Is there anything I do that causes tension or makes you feel isolated?
29. In what ways can I better handle and resolve conflicts between us?
30. Do you feel secure in our relationship?

Relationships are not always smooth sailing; there are ups and downs, tears and laughter, and victories and losses. Marriage is a commitment to your partner that you will weather out whatever challenges come your way. Here are 32 questions that can help you reconnect with your partner in times of disconnect.

1. What is the physical feature you love most about me?
2. Which trait of mine do you love most?
3. Is there any part of yourself that you wish were different?
4. If you had three wishes from a genie, what would you use those wishes on?
5. If you have the opportunity to have a new career, what would you choose?
6. When you hear the word "retirement," what do you picture?
7. Where do you see our marriage in five years?
8. Where do you see our marriage in 10 years?
9. What motto do you live by?

10. Which TV show or movie character do you relate to the most?
11. If a biography or movie were to be made about you, what would its title be and which actor would play your part?
12. What is your favorite part of the day?
13. Do I have a hobby or quirk that you find annoying?
14. How would you describe our relationship using only three words?
15. If given the chance, what aspects of our wedding day would you change?
16. When did you first realize you were in love with me?
17. When did you realize you wanted to marry me?
18. What is your favorite part about being married?
19. As a kid, did you have any fantasies or visions about how your wedding would go?
20. What makes you the most excited for the future?
21. What topics are off-limits for jokes and ribs?
22. If someone invested in you to start a business, what would your business be about?
23. What are some of the things you are most thankful for?
24. Between your parents, which of them do you think you're most like?
25. What is one thing you will never tolerate from me or anyone else?
26. What have you learned in previous relationships that helped you become a better partner?
27. What makes you feel proud of yourself?
28. How is your relationship with your family currently?

29. How is your relationship with my side of the family currently?
30. What is something you never meant to do but worked out well for you in the end anyway?
31. What is your favorite memory from our relationship before we got married?
32. Growing up, which public figure did you most look up to?

Questions to Bring Something New into the Marriage

In married life, you and your partner will inevitably settle into habits and routines. Part of keeping any relationship healthy is doing something different and having some fun every once in a while. Here are 18 questions to see what new adventure you can bring to the table.

1. If we were to get matching tattoos, what design would you propose?
2. Do you have anything new you want to try in bed?
3. Do you have something you wish we did differently in bed?
4. What item on your bucket list do you want to check off the most?
5. Is there a home renovation or remodelling project you want to start?
6. Would you like to go on a cross-country road trip?
7. Do you want to have dinner in that newly opened restaurant in town?
8. Is there a tradition from your childhood or your culture that you want to integrate into our lives?
9. Is there a new activity or hobby that you want to try together?
10. Do you think we should adopt a pet?

11. Do you think it's time for us to move to a new home?
12. Do you want to renew our vows?
13. If we had an entire week off to do anything we want and go wherever we want, what would our itinerary look like?
14. Do you have an idea for a date that we haven't tried yet?
15. Do you want to hold another type of wedding ceremony?
16. Are there any goals you want to set for our marriage?
17. For you, what do you think would bring more excitement into our marriage?
18. Is there any achievement or milestone you want to splurge on a celebration for?"

[Source:https://weddingfrontier.com/questions-to-ask-your-spouse-to-improve-your-marriage/

A Step-by-Step Guide to Fix and Save a Broken Marriage - Clinically Approved by Angela Welch, LMFT| By Callen Winslow, Author - Updated: 16 Jan, 2024

"It's a horrible feeling when you recognize that things aren't working in your marriage. A failing marriage is the worst relationship catastrophe that you can imagine. It leaves a trail of pain, anguish, and disenchantment.

You want to be together and fix and save a broken marriage but feel that there is too much broken trust to make that happen.

Have you ever asked yourself how to fix a broken marriage?

Restoring a broken marriage isn't easy, but it's not impossible. Through careful steps and understanding why marriages end up broken, you would be able to start working on your relationship before it's too late.

How to fix and save a broken marriage: A step-by-step guide

Fixing a broken marriage can be a challenging journey, but it's a path that can lead to rekindling the flames of love. In this step-by-step guide, we'll walk you through the process of rebuilding a bond that may have weathered storms.

It's a journey that demands effort, understanding, and the courage to heal and grow together. Here's a step-by-step guide to help you fix and save a broken marriage

Step 1: Heartfelt conversations

Start by talking openly with your partner. Share your feelings and listen to their perspective. Create a safe space for dialogue.

Step 2: Professional guidance

Seek the support of a qualified therapist or counsellor to fix and save a broken marriage. They can offer valuable insights and guide you through the process.

Step 3: Uncover the roots

Together, dig deep to understand the underlying issues in your marriage. Identify what led to the break and what needs mending.

Step 4: Reconnect and rebuild

Invest in quality time, emotional intimacy, trust-building, and personal growth. Rebuild your marriage one step at a time with patience and commitment.

How to save your marriage: 10 essential tips

If you are wondering about how to fix a marriage or relationship, you need to take a step back, reflect, and consider what is truly wrong and then try out these ways on how to rekindle a marriage.

1. Identify what made you fall in love

It's heart-breaking when you think about how madly you were in love with your partner and how damaged your relationship has gotten.

If you are thinking about how to fix and save a broken marriage or how to mend a broken relationship, get back to basics and put yourself into the mindset of when you were first together and first in love.

Think about what made you fall in love with one another and maybe even write it down.

Consider what you adored about this person and what made you want to be with them.

Though you may have lost sight of this, thinking back to when times were good and you had just fallen in love can help lift your spirits and heal your broken marriage.

Recommended – Save My Marriage Course

Write down their best traits, and you may even find that they are still there, but you've had a hard time getting in touch with them lately.

2. Start to listen to each other again

Have conversations again and start to communicate with one another. Listen to what your spouse is telling you, and then ask the same from them.

Make it a point to listen to one another again, and it may very well be what helps you uncover what was once great about your marriage.

Wondering how to make a marriage work? Just listen to your partner, try to understand what he or she needs. This is one of the most important things you can do to fix and save a broken marriage.

Listening is powerful! Listening carefully will help you save your marriage.

3. Reflect on what has made your marriage feel broken

Why do marriages fail? Where did things go wrong? What happened that got you to the point of a broken marriage? Have you grown apart? Did one of you cheat? Or did life get in the way?

Identifying the causes of a broken marriage is important to fix one.

Even if a relationship has gone through such problems, saving a broken marriage is not impossible.

Think of when things went from good to bad, and then try to find a solution to fix a broken relationship or fix a broken marriage.

4. Talk to each other

Be patient with one another, even in the areas that present the biggest problems. This can be really helpful in your quest to fix and save a broken marriage.

A study establishes the fact that an increase in liking between individuals was correlated with an increase in patience.

Talk to one another rather than at one another. This is part of listening, for when you increase communication, it helps you connect again.

Be patient and willing to work through the problems and know that it will lead you to better times. This is a critical issue to consider when saving your marriage from falling apart.

5 Easy and Effective Couples Communication Tips

Don't let distractions get in the way of your relationship

Sure, you may have kids and careers and many other things in your life, but don't let them stand in the way of your marriage.

Life gets busy, but a couple must grow together and align throughout the good and bad times.

Make it a point to date again, talk more, and ensure that you are still a unified source no matter how busy life may get.

Keep dating your partner, and dating is the key to save a broken marriage.

It helps to fix and save a broken marriage because as you schedule dates to meet each other with a free mind, you can keep yourselves accountable to one another.

6. Find a way to connect again

Think of what it would take to connect once again.

Plan a trip for just the two of you. Commit to spending even a few minutes together every night chatting. Go out on dates and make each other a priority.

When you feel disconnected, here are great ways to reconnect with your spouse with the help of Avital or "The Parenting Junkie," founder of Present Play.

7. Commit to each other

Fixing a broken marriage is never easy.

Aside from trying, you also have to commit, and most of the time, this is where everything goes wrong.

Some people have a hard time committing, and this causes further problems. Learning how to repair a broken marriage starts with commitment.

8. Fix yourself first

When thinking of how to mend a broken marriage, remember that healing a broken marriage starts with us.

It's easier to point fingers and list all the things your partner lacks, but marriage isn't like that.

If you want to fix what's broken in your marriage, you also need to reflect on yourself and work on it first.

We're not perfect, but if you are both willing to work on yourselves first, then on your marriage, it will work out.

Remember, you should be sure of yourself and be complete so that your partner won't have to carry your weight in the relationship.

9. List all your spouse's positive traits and appreciate

"I want to know how to fix my marriage, but my spouse is always making mistakes!"

There's one way to learn how to fix a broken marriage, and that is through listing your spouse's positive traits.

Of course, this will depend on the reason your marriage is on the rocks. If it were because of infidelity or abuse, this tip wouldn't apply.

If your broken marriage was because of differences in priorities, crisis, poor communication, or even about money, you could still use this technique.

List all the positive traits of your spouse.

Your spouse might not align with your priorities, but he is a good cook, he works hard, you feel his love, and he doesn't drink or smoke.

We focus too much on what we can't see rather than the things that we do.

If you can appreciate the things that your spouse can do, it will be easier to make an effort and find ways how to restore a broken marriage.

10. Get to know each other again

A lot of women wonder, "How to fix my marriage with my husband?" Busy routines are a big factor behind this.

Because of our hectic schedule, kids, and stress, we wake up one day and we don't know our spouse the way we used to.

Learn how to save a marriage that is falling apart by committing that you will understand each other more.

Get to know each other again. Learn what makes your spouse inspired, their goals, and what they don't like. Getting to know each other again will help you understand where both of you are coming from.

How to repair a broken marriage: 7 things that you can do

When a marriage hits rocky shores, it's not the end of the story; it's the beginning of a new chapter. Repairing a broken marriage takes time, dedication, and love.

Here are 7 simple things you can do to rekindle the love when wondering how to rebuild a marriage:

- Start with a heart-to-heart conversation where both partners express their feelings and concerns openly.
- Dedicate undistracted time to be together, whether it's a date night or simply sharing a cup of coffee.

- Rediscover the physical and emotional connection that first brought you together.
- To move forward, forgive each other for past mistakes and release grudges.
- Consider couples therapy or counselling to navigate difficult issues with the guidance of an expert.
- Work on personal growth and self-awareness to be the best partner you can be.
- Both partners must commit to making the necessary changes and putting in the effort to repair the marriage.

How to fix a broken marriage with counselling

How do you fix a broken marriage when you and your spouse are almost giving up? This is where counselling helps.

Marriage and couple counselling can make a huge difference in your quest to fix your marriage.

Counselling, through the guidance of a licensed therapist, can help you and your spouse work through your issues and strengthen your bond.

First and foremost, it's essential to acknowledge the need for professional help and then choose a counsellor you both feel comfortable with. You can look for feasible and effective 'marriage counselling near me'.

During counselling sessions, it's essential to be open and honest. Share your thoughts, emotions, and concerns freely.

The work doesn't end in the counsellor's office. Be prepared to do the homework and put what you've learned into practice in your daily life. As your marriage begins to mend, focus on rebuilding emotional intimacy and trust, as these are often at the core of a healthy and thriving partnership.

Commonly asked questions

Marriage isn't always a smooth sail, and it's okay to seek guidance when needed. Here are answers to some frequently asked questions about recognizing issues, managing conflicts, and seeking professional help in a struggling marriage.

What are the signs of a broken marriage?

Signs of a struggling marriage can vary, but common indicators include lack of communication, constant arguing, emotional distance, infidelity, or a feeling of unhappiness. If you sense a disconnect or ongoing unhappiness, it may be a sign your marriage needs attention.

How to manage conflict in a relationship?

Conflict is natural, but how you handle it matters. Try active listening, open communication, and a willingness to compromise. Address the issue, not the person, and remember you're a team working toward a solution. Seek to understand each other's perspectives.

How to seek professional help for a broken marriage?

Seeking professional help is a positive step. You can start by researching marriage counsellors or therapists in your area. Choose someone you both feel comfortable with. Reach out to them for an initial consultation to discuss your needs and expectations.

Saving your marriage in time

When you can find your way back to one another again and reconnect, it may help fix a broken marriage.

These suggestions on how to save a marriage and how to deal with a broken marriage will surely help you salvage your relationship.

Sometimes it's a matter of reflecting upon things that will help you find lasting happiness, even when you think that the marriage is falling apart—this is how to make a broken marriage work and enjoy that happily ever after that you always dreamed of!" [Source: https://www.marriage.com/advice/save-your-marriage/6-ways-to-successfully-fix-save-a-broken-marriage/]

10 Effects of Divorce on Children — and Helping Them Cope

Splitting up isn't easy. Entire novels and pop songs have been written about it. And when children are involved, divorce can be an especially sensitive situation.

Breathe. You're in the right place. The truth is that divorce does impact kids — sometimes in ways you wouldn't quite expect. But it isn't all doom and gloom.

If you're feeling overwhelmed, remind yourself that you're doing what's right for you and your family. Moving forward, try your very best to plan, understand the potential warning signs, and make yourself emotionally available to your child.

That all said, let's jump in with some ways your child may express their feelings surrounding separation.

1. They feel angry

Kids may feel angry about divorce. If you think about it, it makes sense. Their whole world is changing — and they don't necessarily have much input. Anger can strike at any age, but it's particularly present with school-aged kids and teens. These emotions may arise from feelings of abandonment or loss of control. Anger may even be directed inward, as some children blame themselves for their parents' divorce.

2. They may withdraw socially

You may also notice that your social butterfly child has become quite shy or anxious. They're likely thinking about and feeling a lot right now. They may seem uninterested or even fearful of social situations, like hanging out with friends or attending school events.

Low self-image is associated with both divorce and social withdrawal, so boosting your child's confidence and inner dialogue may help them come out of their shell again.

3. Their grades might suffer

Academically, kids going through divorce may earn lower grades and even face a higher dropout rate compared to their peers. These effects may be seen as early as age 6 but may be more noticeable as kids reach the ages of 13 to 18 years old.

There are several possible reasons for this link, including that children may feel neglected, depressed, or distracted by increased conflict between their parents. With time, less interest in academics at the high school level may trickle over to less interest with furthering their education overall.

4. They feel separation anxiety

Younger children may show signs of separation anxiety, such as increased crying or clinginess. Of course, this is also a developmental milestone that tends to begin between the ages of 6 to 9 months and resolve by 18 months.

Still, older toddlers and kids may show signs of separation anxiety or may ask for the other parent when they're not around.

Some kids may respond well to consistent routine as well as visual tools, such as a calendar, with visitations clearly labelled on it.

5. Little ones may regress

Toddlers and pre-schoolers between the ages of 18 months and 6 years old may revert back to behaviors like clinginess, bedwetting, thumb sucking, and temper tantrums.

If you notice regression, it may be a sign of increased stress on your child or their difficulty with transition. These behaviors can be worrisome — and you may not know where to start with helping your little one. The keys here are continual reassurance and consistency in the environment — actions that make your child feel safe.

6. Their eating and sleeping patterns change

One 2019 study poses the question of whether or not children literally carry the weight of divorce. While body mass index (BMI) in kids doesn't immediately show an impact, the BMI over time may be "significantly" higher than children who haven't gone through divorce. And these effects are particularly noted in kids who experience separation before turning 6 years old.

Children in most age groups also encounter sleep issues, which may contribute to weight gain. This goes back to regression, but also includes things like nightmares or belief in monsters or other fantastical beings that bring about feelings of anxiety around bedtime.

7. They may pick sides

When parents fight, research explains that children go through both cognitive dissonance and loyalty conflict. This is just a fancy way of saying that they feel uncomfortable being stuck in the middle, not knowing if they should side with one parent over another.

This may show up as an intense need for "fairness" even if it's harmful to their own development. Kids may also show their discomfort with increased stomach-aches or headaches.

The loyalty conflict may become even more pronounced as children get older, eventually leading to a total break in contact with one parent (though the chosen parent may change with time).

8. They go through depression

While a child may initially feel low or sad about the divorce, studies report that children of divorce are at risk of developing clinical depression. Even more concerning, a few are also at higher risk of suicide threats or attempts.

While these issues can impact kids of any age, they tend to be more prominent with kids ages 11 years and older. And boys may be more at risk of suicidal thoughts than girls, according to the American Academy of Paediatrics.

Enlisting the help of a licensed mental health professional is critically important for this reason.

9. They engage in risky behaviors

Abuse of alcohol and drugs, aggressive behavior, and early introduction to sexual activity are also possible. For example, studies show that teen girls tend to have sex at earlier ages when they live in a household where the father isn't present.

Research does not show the same risk for boys. And this early "sexual debut" may be attributed to several factors, including modified beliefs about marriage and thoughts on childbearing.

10. They face their own relationship struggles

Finally, studies show that when parents' divorce, there's a good chance that their kids could wind up in the same position as adults. The idea here is that a split between parents may change a child's attitude toward relationships in general. They may be less enthused to enter long-term, committed relationships.

And living through divorce shows kids that there are many alternatives to family models. The research also suggests that children may choose cohabitation (living together without being married) over marriage. However, it's worth noting that this is fairly normalized in our current culture, regardless of family history.

Helping your kids cope

Things can get tough and touchy in even the most cooperative of split-ups. Divorce isn't an easy topic to broach. But your children will appreciate your transparency and understanding of their stake in the situation.

Some other tips to help them cope:

- **Encourage your child to talk to you.** Explain that you're a safe place to share any feelings they might be having. Then, most importantly, listen with open ears to anything they have to say.
- **Understand that all kids process change differently.** What works for one of your kids may not speak to another. Pay attention to any acting out or other cues you see, and pivot your approach accordingly.
- **Try to eliminate conflict between yourself and your ex if possible (and it may not always be possible).** When parents fight in front of their kids, it has the potential to result in "taking sides" or loyalty to one parent over another. (By the way, this isn't a divorce phenomenon. It happens with kids of married couples who fight, too.)
- **Reach out for help if you need it.** This may be in the form of your own family and friends support system. But if your child is starting to display some warning signs, call your paediatrician or a mental

health professional. You don't need to face things alone.

- **Be kind to yourself.** Yes, your child needs you to be strong and centered. Still, you're only human. It's perfectly fine and even encouraged to show emotions in front of your kids. Showing your own emotions will likely help your children open up about their own as well............................" **[Source: https://www.healthline.com/health/parenting/effects-of-divorce-on-children]**

Important Environmental Factors That Influence Early Childhood Development by Mahak Arora - Updated: December 7, 2023: [Source: firstcry Parenting Website]

"A child's development is intricately shaped by a myriad of factors, intricately interwoven with the delicate dance of nature and nurture. Unveiling the layers of these influences enables parents to adeptly navigate their child's needs. The child's growth is profoundly affected by the environment they are immersed in—the attention and affection bestowed by parents, and the daily acceptance within the familial framework. Moreover, the cumulative impact of the child's overall diet emerges as a pivotal influence on their life trajectory. Delving deeper into this discourse unravels insights into the paramount role of the environment in child development, offering a roadmap for parents to provide optimal support.

Areas of Child Development

Child development is a dynamic and multifaceted process encompassing various domains that shape a child's growth. Understanding these areas is crucial for parents and caregivers to provide holistic support. We'll now explore five key domains that play pivotal roles in a child's overall well-being and progress.

1. Intellectual Development

Intellectual development refers to a child's cognitive growth, encompassing aspects such as problem-solving, memory, language acquisition, and critical thinking. Stimulating activities, educational games, and exposure to diverse experiences contribute to robust cognitive development.

2. Physical Development

Physical development involves the enhancement of gross and fine motor skills, coordination, and overall physical fitness. Adequate nutrition, regular exercise, and a safe environment foster optimal physical growth, ensuring a child's well-being.

3. Emotional Development

Emotional development pertains to a child's ability to form relationships, understand emotions, and regulate their own feelings. Positive interactions, emotional support, and opportunities for social engagement contribute to healthy social-emotional development.

4. Social Development

Social development is crucial for effective communication and expression. Reading, storytelling, and encouraging verbal interactions aid in language acquisition. Providing a rich linguistic environment fosters vocabulary expansion and language fluency.

5. Moral Development

Moral development encompasses a child's evolving identity, self-esteem, and social awareness. Nurturing a positive self-image, fostering a sense of belonging, and encouraging autonomy contribute to robust psychosocial development.

Understanding and actively supporting these five areas of child development lay the foundation for a well-rounded and thriving individual.

What Role Does a Child's Environment Play in Their Development?

A child's environment plays a pivotal role in their development, influencing various aspects of their growth. The environment includes physical surroundings, family dynamics, socio-economic conditions, and cultural influences. A supportive and stimulating environment fosters cognitive, emotional, and social development. Conversely, adverse conditions may hinder growth, highlighting the significance of creating a positive, nurturing space for optimal child development.

Environmental Factors Affecting Child Development

Some of the factors that affect child development are:

1. Family and Bonding

One of the most important influencing factors on your child's development is his/her family. Irrespective of who is your child's primary caregiver – you and your spouse, older siblings, or relatives – the bonding provided within a family home helps nurture and protect your child physically and emotionally? Parents who spend quality time with their children create a secure bond with their children and hence the child grows with secure attachment and confidence (2). The time you invest in nurturing your child will show in his/her positive development and growth. There are several things you can do to bond better with your child. You can make it a point to read to him regularly, thus establishing a routine and helping both of you bond with each other. Playing with your child is important as well, both in establishing a close relationship as well as in helping him develop their motor skills. You can also simply talk to your child, be it about your day or theirs, showing them that his/her inputs and opinions are valuable to you.

In contrast, children who are abused or neglected by their families suffer in terms of their mental and emotional well-being. These things include corporal punishment and verbal insults, and indifference. Leaving a child to watch TV the whole day without opportunities for genuine human interaction will prevent him from getting the required experience required to develop and prevent early speech development in children.

Finally, it is important to know that maintaining a good relationship with your child is important but not enough. The entire family needs to be cohesive and protective of each other (3). For instance, children raised by parents who argue or fight consistently grow up having problems building friendships and relationships. Also, caring for all your children equally and paying them the same amount of attention will make them develop a sense of fairness and camaraderie.

2. Physical Environment

The effect of the environment on child development cannot be understated, and this includes the physical surroundings they are raised in. If your living environment is cramped, noisy and filled with aggression, your child's personality can be affected. If you have too many people living at home and if the attention towards him is divided, he may seek out alternative forms of attention which can lead to an emotional distance between him/her and you. Similarly, unpleasant surroundings often cause children to block out or bury negativity, making them more introverted.

School is an important part of a child's life considering how much time he spends there every day. As a parent, it is your responsibility to identify which school is most suited to your child's needs. Further, keeping yourself updated with your child's school activities, meeting his teachers regularly and interacting with his peers and their parents is the mark of a good, concerned parent.

You can also enrol your child in enrichment courses like martial arts programmes, meditation, music classes, and so on, depending on your budget. Many community-specific organisations offer these programmes at affordable rates. This is even more important in today's time owing to the dependence on technology and the internet.

3. Financial Situation

It's not a surprise that money is a deciding factor when it comes to living comfortably. It has been well established that the privilege of wealth is real and that it has a greater impact on childhood development than education. For instance, rich parents can afford to spend more time with their children and poorer parents are too caught up in making ends meet to have the privilege of quality time. Wealth also helps secure better academic training, opportunities for travel, extra classes, and so on (4).

It's easy to forget that money is not sufficient to provide for a child; you have to be deeply involved in his life. You can start by explaining to your child how money and budgets work in a way he can understand. Tell your child that he will always be taken care of, even if things are rough.

Children can thrive in a less well-to-do family as long as they are loved and wanted. Remember that children are more influenced by the quality of time you spend with them and not the quantity. Your child may not remember how much money you spent on his education, but he will remember if you turned up to his annual school functions or supported him when he won a prize or celebrated when he came first in class. You don't have to do much to show your child you care; simply sharing a meal with him every night is enough for your little one to feel secure and happy.

4. Health and Nutrition

Nutrition is crucial for the physical and mental growth of a child. A balanced diet is also required by pregnant women as malnutrition can lead to problems like low birth weight, miscarriages, stillbirths, slowed development, and so on. In children, habits like unhealthy or excessive eating can lead to weight gain, obesity, diabetes, stunted growth, lethargy, and a host of other complications.

Infants thrive on breast milk – the ideal food consisting of carbs, fats, proteins, minerals, vitamins, antibodies, and everything else growing new-born needs. Breastfed babies are less likely to become obese, have low levels of cholesterol, and improved cognition. After the first six months, you can complement your child's diet with solid foods. Ensure that your child is getting micronutrients such as vitamin A, iodine, and iron, as the lack of these can cause serious problems like vision defects, goitre, cretinism, anaemia, and so on. These problems have been linked to reduced motor skills and social development of toddlers and young children.

5. Learning

In addition to learning at school, make sure that your home environment also stimulates your child's mental development. This includes cognitive, linguistic, emotional, and motor skills. The best environment for this is a calm and loving home that allows your child to focus on improving his abilities. The absence of such a stimulating environment can have a negative impact on your child's language and speech development. Not having a positive environment for learning can cause anxiety, absence of stimulation, not wanting to stay in one place for too long, and so on.

You should make an effort to create opportunities for your child to explore his interests, especially at home. Instil a sense of curiosity in your child, encourage him to question everything and teach him to find solutions by himself.

Some important ways you can create a positive atmosphere for your child are:

Use positive words of affirmation.

Go for critique instead of criticism.

Always apologise for your mistakes, and allow your child to do the same.

Solve the problem at hand immediately, and don't let it fester.

Show affection and warmth.

Limit electronics to at least an hour each day and spend quality time.

Practice what you preach, and your child will follow.

6. Social Media and Television

In the realm of virtual platforms encompassing social media and television, an escalation in screen time is becoming increasingly common. Children, akin to absorbent sponges, look up to their parents as early-life role models. It is imperative to avoid conveying the message that smartphones or laptops hold superiority over the offline world. To employ these media forms constructively, limit their use to recommended periods, ensuring the content aligns with educational and age-appropriate standards during children's screen time if complete avoidance is not feasible. A related survey conducted on US adults divulges diverse parental strategies for digital discipline. Further insights are presented in the accompanying graph.

Roughly eight-in-ten or more parents limit when and how long their child can use screens or digitally 'ground' their child

% of U.S. parents of a child age 5 to 11 who say they ...

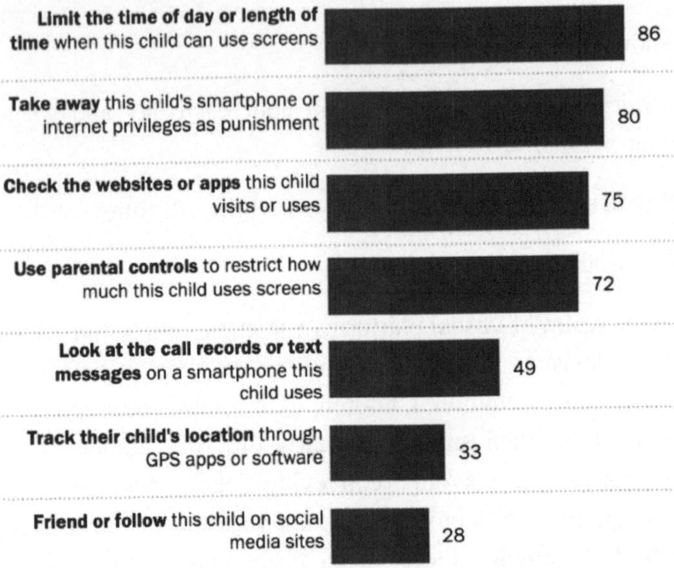

Note: If parent has multiple children, they were asked to focus on one child when answering this question. Those who did not give an answer or who gave other responses are not shown.
Source: Survey of U.S. adults conducted March 2-15, 2020.
"Parenting Children in the Age of Screens"

PEW RESEARCH CENTER

FAQs

1. At What Age Do Environmental Factors Have an Impact on a Child's Development?

Environmental factors can influence a child's development from infancy. The early years, particularly the first three, are crucial as the brain undergoes rapid growth and development. However, environmental factors continue to shape a child's development throughout their formative years.

2. Impact of Growing Up in an Unstable Home Environment on a Child's Development?

Growing up in an unstable home environment can have profound and lasting effects on a child's development. It may lead to emotional, behavioural, and academic challenges, impacting their overall well-being. The instability can manifest in issues like anxiety, low self-esteem, and difficulty forming secure relationships.

3. How Can a Child's Mental Health be influenced by Exposure to Violence?

Exposure to violence can significantly impact a child's mental health. It may lead to trauma, anxiety, depression, and behavioural issues. Children exposed to violence may also exhibit difficulties in forming healthy relationships and may struggle with emotional regulation.

4. How Do Parenting Styles Impact a Child's Social and Cognitive Development?

Parenting styles play a crucial role in shaping a child's social and cognitive development. Authoritative parenting, characterized by warmth and reasonable control, tends to foster positive outcomes. Authoritarian or permissive styles may lead to challenges, affecting a child's ability to form relationships, regulate emotions, and perform academically.

As a parent, you must expose your child to the right kind of environment as that will have a direct impact on his behaviour, learning, and personality. There is no manual of parenting which can tell you about the perfect set of opportunities you can provide for your child, but you must try as much as possible to be there for him/her. The key thing to remember is to keep your home environment peaceful and loving, bond with your children, and provide them with the love, affection, attention and acceptance that they need to grow and thrive." [https://parenting.firstcry.com/articles/5-environmental-factors-influencing-early-childhood-development/]

Psycho Social Consequences Of Broken Homes On Children: A Study Of Divorced, Separated, Deserted And Blended Families - March 2020 - Pakistan Journal of Applied Social Sciences 6(1) - DOI:10. 46568/pjass.v6i1.307 – License - CC BY-NC-ND 4.0 - Authors: Ayesha Gul, Muhammad Nadeemullah - Research Gate [Excerpts] :

"Abstract

Home is the first and instantaneous unit for every child. He or she is born into and consider as a full member of the home. Home is a recognized group of people who are joined together by marriage. Children from broken families are about five times more likely to suffer damaging mental problems than those whose parents are together. I have selected this topic because it's a main social issue now days. Since the divorce rate is increasing rapidly, it affects the whole life of individual. The purpose of this research is to trace the effects of broken homes on the psycho, social and academic performances of a child. The researcher practiced snowball sampling in order to get through to their respondents. The total respondents on which this research is done are 170 children under the age group 10 to 18 year and selected through simple probability sampling with use of snowball sampling technique from four of the secondary schools with the help of Questionnaire and Interview Schedule. The study found the situation that the ratio avoid to go school and low grades of girls is higher than boys due to financial burdens as girls engage themselves in different income resources to overcome the financial crises. Study also found that due to aggressive nature, the boy often tend towards disobedience and suffers from anxiety after a series of hopeless thoughts towards tackling the different challenges. The study recommended it is possible to have healthy, adjusted kids after a divorce, and it is also possible to have a solid relationship with your children with lots of time together after divorce. And family researches should be conducted, so the psychologists, psychiatrists, sociologists and economists can more work over divorce and its consequences and for the betterment of the society.................

"...........Conclusion:

It is concluded that family is very important as it shapes our development and personality. The family protects your dignity and takes care of your wellbeing. Family also gives us teachings that guide us throughout our lives and these are the values we carry everywhere we go. In addition, your family comes to your aid during hard times. Family is the building block of a successful person. Family is the first friend; first brick and first memory of a person. It can either make you or break you into pieces. A broken family is typically considered to be a family where one of the parents is missing due to divorce or perhaps the second parent was never part of the family. There are ways to minimize the emotional impact that individual usually feel in these kinds of families. If the single parent really puts forth effort to provide a stable, loving and supportive environment for their individual, it can go a long way to soften the blow of a broken family.

Recommendations:

By taking into consideration the above scenario, certain recommendations to further improve the status of broken families and its victims "specially children" the following recommendation have been put:

- Family researches should be conducted, so the psychologists, psychiatrists, sociologists and economists can more work over divorce and its consequences and for the betterment of the society.
- Children often believe that their parent's separation is their own fault. Therefore, it is important to tell children that they are not the cause of the separation. Parents need to repeat this number of times.
- It is helpful to tell young children that it's normal to not feel good about what is happening, and that's lots of other children feel this way when their parents become separated. It is also okay for parents to share their emotions with children by saying something like "I am having a hard time since the separation, just like you, but I know it's going to get better after a while "And should not criticize the other parent.
- Tell your children that, anytime they want to talk about the separation, to come to you. It is healthy for children to get out their pent-up emotions in

discussions with their parents and to learn that the parents are willing to listen to their feelings and fears.

- Children need parents who care enough to not only give them warmth and nurturance but also set reasonable limits. If children must leave friends behind, it is important for parents to help the children stay in touch by phone or by other mean. Keeping the child busy and involved in the new settings can also keep their minds off the stressful thoughts about the separation.
- After a divorce or separation, parents are as important to children as before the divorce or separation. Divorced parents need to provide children with as much support as possible. Divorced parents can find people who provide practical help and with whom they can talk about their problems. However, seeking out others for support and feedback about problems can make the transition to a single parent family more bearable.
- It is important that efforts should be made to see that girls particularly in their adolescence are given the necessary education to play their role effectively as wife, mother and other interrelated relations that is the education for family life. Family life education has a distinct socio-physiological connotation and is provided mainly through family counselling and specialized courses.
- Divorced parents are advised to help their children talk about and share-things about each other so that the children can integrate the two parents lives and life style into a whole some, meaningful system of

living. Anger, hurt, jealousy, and other negative emotions may make such an adjustment hard for both adults and children. The divorced father/mother should justify to his/her children that he/she will remain their father/mother regardless of his/her marital status.

- As soon as daily activities in the home make it obvious that one parent is leaving, tell the children. If possible, both parents should be present when the children are made aware of the separation to come. The reasons for the separation are very difficult for young children to understand. No matter what parents tell children, children can find reasons to argue against the separation. It is extremely important for parents to tell the children who will take care of them and to describe the specific arrangements for seeing the other parent.
- Parents should pay attention and provide emotional affection to their kids because whatever time they had to spend enjoying has been passed. It's the children's who have to grow up and suffer.
- Children should be involved in social gathering activities so that their social life would not be affected much.
- Parents should help children to express their feelings verbally and non- Verbally (i.e. art, music, writing)"

"THERE IS A TIME IN OUR LIVES, USUALLY IN MID-LIFE, WHEN A WOMAN HAS TO MAKE A DECISION - POSSIBLY THE MOST IMPORTANT PSYCHIC DECISION OF HER FUTURE LIFE - AND THAT IS, WHETHER TO BE BITTER OR NOT.

WOMEN OFTEN COME TO THIS IN THEIR LATE THIRTIES OR EARLY FORTIES. THEY ARE AT THE POINT WHERE THEY ARE FULL UP TO THEIR EARS WITH EVERYTHING AND THEY'VE "HAD IT" AND "THE LAST STRAW HAS BROKEN THE CAMEL'S BACK" AND THEY'RE "PISSED OFF AND POOPED OUT." THEIR DREAMS OF THEIR TWENTIES MAY BE LYING IN A CRUMPLE. THERE MAY BE BROKEN HEARTS, BROKEN MARRIAGES, BROKEN PROMISES."- CLARISSA PINKOLA ESTES

In situations of the nature noted before, it is important to know why it so happened or made to happen and what would have been missing point in between them. It is always better that partners intending to wedlock make themselves mentally strong to sustain the tie-up and give little room for any kind of mutual suspicion. Mentally strong and resilient people overcome adversities and learn from them. Research finds that mentally resilient people have personality traits that help them cope with adversity. They tend toward emotional maturity and make an effort to process negative events from their past. What does mentally strong mean? In its natural sense, it is a bit difficult to answer this question more lucidly. However, most significant aspect of mentally strong is calmness. Calmness is most powerful spiritual power one who practices it enjoys. Question arises what is practising of calmness. I will come to this point a bit later. Calmness enables to grow within oneself the controlling of mind, courage, conviction and self-control. It births from positivity dominance in the mind. Mind has two characters; one is positivity and second is the negativity. Let me deal first about positivity.

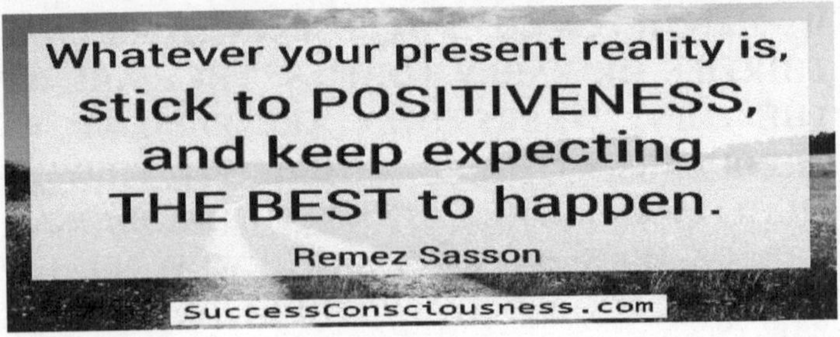

All that lies in the unknown future should be embraced as it comes and enjoy it with positivity in mind. "The mind comprises impulses, feelings, emotions, likes and dislikes. If we are not in control of the mind, we will be controlled by the mind, having life full of endless stress. Many people are living their lives on the past or on the future and are often far away from present. They are either worried about the past or anxious about the future. While preoccupying themselves with their past mistakes and losses or pondering about what tomorrow will bring and how will they survive in the future, they are missing to enjoy life in the present. According to Chinmayananda, brooding over the past is like carrying a dead body on shoulders that keeps the person carrying always in agitating mind. Future is

unknown. The best choice, therefore, is to live in the present. This opens abundant opportunities which we don't want to think about. Adjustment to the present is the life line of the human being for good living of the life.

Question is whether giving weight and attaching importance may be because of failure to get what one wants or failure to achieve adds to the agony. Success comes through failures, what Great men realized and ultimately achieved their goal and earned fame in the world. Let us look at them rather than sitting with soreness. Read their life and achievements to regain self-confidence and sense of positivity. It is said that “To fail is not to succeed, and success is the absence of failure. ... Firstly, failure starts where success ends, and it defines the limits of success. But secondly, success often follows failure, since it frequently occurs after other options have been tried and failed”. It is also said that “Failure won't kill you but your fear to fail just may keep you from success. ... Failure simply means there is something to be learned or another direction to be taken. Here's why failure is GOOD: Failure is a redirection.” Successful people who failed and became renowned in the world: Thomas Edison, Elvis Presley, Michael Jordan, Vincent van Gogh, Stephen King, Fred Astaire, Abraham Lincoln, JK Rowling and Albert Einstein.

Love is not attachment. Love understands sharing; it is feeling peace and harmony in the presence of our spouse. Love has nothing to do with falling in love although this falling in love is being sold to us through movies and literature as something we should strive for. Mind is being granted too much importance and attention. Countless therapies from psychoanalysis to all kinds of self-help practices are developed promising to improve our mind, raise our IQ, teach us how to achieve our goals and satisfy our desires, while the best thing we you can do about our mind is to learn how to ignore it. Vedanta teaches us that even the Scripture shouldn’t be accepted if we find it to be contrary to our perception, to our common sense. In living our life, try to be objective, try looking things from outside and above, as impartial observer. Examine the motives of our actions. Are we acting based on our likes and dislikes? Desires? Learn to recognize chaotic impulses of the mind and stay above it; refuse to obey it. Ignore the noise which is telling us that we should be like everybody else.

Bad blood is a feeling of ill will, anger, or hostility between people. When there's bad blood, people aren't getting along. Besides its literal meaning, the word blood has long been used to refer to people's emotions. ... Bad blood tends to make people hot-blooded: angry. Bad blood is considered to cause, among others, the Blood Pressure. ....Negative attitudes and feelings of helplessness and hopelessness can create chronic stress, which upsets the body's hormone balance, depletes the brain chemicals required for happiness, and damages the immune system. Chronic stress can actually decrease our lifespan. Our thoughts and emotions can affect our health. Emotions that are freely experienced and expressed without judgment or attachment tend to flow fluidly without impacting our health. On the other hand, repressed emotions (especially fearful or negative ones) can zap mental energy, negatively affect the body, and lead to health problems. It's important to recognize our thoughts and emotions and be aware of the effect they have—not only on each other, but also on our bodies, behaviour, and relationships." (Source: Taking Charge of your Health Wellbeing – posted on website)

"Anger, fear, resentment, frustration and anxiety are emotional states that many people experience regularly but try to avoid. And this is understandable—they are designed to make us uncomfortable. These negative emotional states can create extra stress in your body and your mind, which is uncomfortable but also can lead to health issues if the stress becomes chronic or overwhelming. Nobody likes to feel uncomfortable, so it is natural to want to escape these feelings, and the dangers of unmanaged stress are real. However, there is a feeling that people sometimes have that these emotions will last forever or that the feelings themselves are the problem.

More often, these feelings are beneficial because they can also send us messages. Anger and anxiety, for example, show that something needs to change, and perhaps that our well-being has been threatened. Fear is an appeal to increase your level of safety. Resentment motivates us to change something in a relationship. Frustration does as well. Basically, negative emotions are there to alert us that something needs to change and to motivate us to make that change.

Swami Vivekananda-How to stop Negative Thoughts:

"How do I stop my negative thoughts?" – is a question that I have been asked many times. If you have ever asked this question then you will feel such enormous relief in knowing the answer, because it is so simple. How do you stop negative thoughts? You plant good thoughts! When you try to stop negative thoughts, you are focusing on what you don't want – negative thoughts – and you will attract an abundance of them. They can never disappear if you are focused on them. The "stop" part is irrelevant – the negative thoughts are your focus It doesn't matter if you are trying to stop negative thoughts or control them or push them away, the result is the same. Your focus is on negative thoughts, and by the law of attraction you are inviting more of them to you.

The truth is always simple and it is always easy. To stop negative thoughts, just plant good thoughts! Deliberately plant good thoughts! You plant good thoughts by making it a daily practice to appreciate all the things in your day. Appreciate your health, your car, your home, your family, your job, your friends, your surroundings, your meals, your pets, and the magnificent beauty of the day. Compliment, praise, and give thanks to all things. Every time you say "Thank you" it is a good thought! As you plant more and better thoughts, the negative thoughts will be wiped out. Why? Because your focus is on good thoughts, and what you focus on you attract.

So don't give any attention to negative thoughts. Don't worry about them. If any come, make light of them, shrug them off, and let them be your reminder to deliberately think more good thoughts now.

The more good thoughts you can plant in a day, the faster your life will be utterly transformed into all good. If you spend only one day speaking of good things and saying "Thank you" at every single opportunity, you will not believe your tomorrow. Deliberately thinking good thoughts is exactly like planting seeds. As you think good thoughts you are planting good seeds inside you, and the Universe will transform those seeds into a garden of paradise. How will the garden of paradise appear? As your life!

Whatever you think, that you will be. If you think yourselves weak, weak you will be; if you think yourselves strong, strong you will be; if you think yourselves impure, impure you will be; if you think yourselves pure, pure you will be. This teaches us not to think ourselves as weak, but

as strong, omnipotent, and omniscient. – Swami Vivekananda" (Source: Website)

Now, I wish to touch my personal views gained through my life of eighty seven years. Negativity of mind resulting, in many cases, into depression, calls for an earnest intervention by virtue of experience, witness to the sufferings, readiness to share other's sadness equally as of one's own, extending help of whatever kind and standing along invigorating spirit of positivity blinded by the negativity, helping those undergoing the torments of negativity and depression. Causes of negativity and depression are explained earlier. Cures for them are also explained earlier. All these are from those learned, researchers and spiritual leaders expressed through their writings for the benefit of those affected. I have presented them above being, in my view, prominently appealing and awakening. This is one part. Other part is translating them into reality by the humans having such problems in life and how best they make use of them. It doesn't end there. It ends when such humans should rebel against negativity imposed upon them to relieve from its pains. The word 'rebel' used invokes a sense of strong mental and physical strength to decisively fight the cause that shows a semblance of authoritarian and dictator in the governing system. Formation of negativity and depression in the mind may be one or many negative reasons happened or happening in one's life. One who has developed such formation in mind is more prone to accord importance and focus thereon which then assumes the character of an 'object' seeking always for focus either how to survive or how to get away. Recognition so attached to the object opens up a locked box having so much of hidden events of life that start flaming up with burning sensation in the mind and body.

I sincerely appeal to those thus affected is not to give any focus to the object encountered in life and never allow that object to stick in the mind by itself as an object. This does not call for great efforts. It is simpler. So many things happen in life, hang and pass away of their own. Never try to stop them. Try to face them as they come and think giving self-confidence, reasoning and control more dominance to overcome when something starts troubling. Get out of that dangerous trap surfacing around and stand firmly on the ground; it is bound to go of its own when it is not focussed and get exhausted of its own. Whatever could be the oncoming cause, build up strong confidence within with determination to overlook it, howsoever serious it may be and wait for the good things to emerge to make life worth living.

It is the natural process in any one's life to come across quarrels, provocations, threatening, browbeating, mistreating, betrayal of trust and challenges and so on, face them with full self-confidence and positivity which prevents formation of any negativity. Some source living on the earth comes to help if one's intent is to avoid negativity honestly and with all the self-belief. One is not alone on Earth. There is Living God in everyone, that is the bestowment of Atman (Soul) and one of everyone would be there to help representing the Spirit of the Soul. Absolute Belief that one would cross over the hurdle is the essence and existence of life. That is the greatest strength and that one should realize. Focus only on Self (Soul) within with all humbleness and gratitude. Self-prevention is better than searching for cure from somewhere that costs unsure of relief. Never lose confidence which acts as a strongest stone to stand and those who try to hit it hurts his own fingers. That should be the spirit of life.

I wish to deal about the suicide which was earlier believed to happen in the mid or later age of human life but is now happening among the teens and the adolescents. It is difficult to pinpoint precisely what could be the cause for leaping towards the suicide. It is also difficult to measure the mind of the person intend to commit suicide. In general, suicide is the act of intentionally causing one's own death.

... The most commonly used method of suicide varies between countries, and is partly related to the availability of effective means. Suicide often stems from a deep feeling of depression and hopelessness. The inability to see solutions to problems or to cope with challenging life circumstances may lead people to see taking their own lives as the only solution to what is really a temporary situation, and most survivors of suicide attempts go on to live full, rewarding lives. Depression is a key risk factor for suicide; others include psychiatric disorders, substance use, chronic pain, a family history of suicide, and a prior suicide attempt. Impulsiveness often plays a role among adolescents who take their life. In my view, the depression/hopelessness originate when the negativity prompts one to presume to be so and makes one to stop there.

It should not be so for; in one’s mind, there is also positivity besides negativity. When one is faced with negativity, one should not stop there regardless of whatever activation and provocation. Few minutes of pause evokes the desire to live that is the birth of positivity. It is the determinant factor to live. See the world around. Those who appreciate the life and living prevailed over the negativity by positivity and continued to enjoy life. The Atman or Soul does not belong to body but body belongs to the Atman or Soul. Atman or Soul leaves the body when one's life time comes to an end. Soul is not dependent on body; Body is dependent on Soul. The body cannot exert any pressure or control over the Soul because it is 'ONE WITHIN ITSELF'. So also the human as the say goes 'YOUR ARE ONE WITHIN YOU; THAT ONENESS IS NOT INDEPENDENT BUT CONNECTED TO SOUL'. "ONE IS THE INTEGRATION OF BODY AND SELF (SOUL)".

Therefore, one should not assume one is free to disintegrate itself from SOUL AND Mother Earth. This means one wants to LEAVE BODILY BEFORE THE LIFE TIME TO COME TO AN END WHICH AMOUNTS TO BETRAYEL OF SOUL AND THE PURPOSE FOR WHICH ONE IS BORN ON EARTH. THIS HAPPENS WHEN ONE CONSIDERS BUBBLE AS GREATER THAN THE OCEAN.

One should think this holy aspect of life first before embarking upon even to think anything about suicide leave apart committing suicide. This is the fact of the life and to be so taken by everyone, more so, by those who are captured by negativity. Negativity should be taken as a bubble in ocean and is bound to burst any time; once it bursts it merges with the ocean. The bubble can be held in hand for few seconds and not beyond that. So also the negativity which is a bubble in the ocean of mind, disappears itself after few seconds or minutes. When one tries to stop the bubble in mind, it cannot, by law of nature, be stopped. It is bound to burst. If one continues to presume that the bubble exists, even there being none, it formats in mind and makes one to invite negativity. How can one say there is something he or she holding in hand when there is nothing in the hand. This is, at best, be called as imagination. When one sticks to the imagination with closed eyes, he or she thereby fails to know what is brightness of imaginative life because imagination is greater than knowledge.

"There is a difference between optimism and stupidity. Optimism is the belief that things will get better. Stupidity is the belief that they will get better without any effort on your part. – **Albert Einstein**

To live is positivity; it is not a bubble but body connected to Soul breakable only as per the ordain of the Soul. What one is doing is right or wrong does not rest on Soul but rests on the Spirit of Conscience that is linked to the Soul. It is necessary to consult the Conscience first. Also, 'YOU ARE NOT ONE ON EARTH; BEHIND YOU, THERE IS A LINE UP OF FAMILY, RELATIVES, FRIENDS, LOVED ONES AND CHILDREN. REMEMBER YOUR ATTACHMENT WITH EACH ONE OF THEM AND DON'T LEAVE THE EARTH OF YOUR OWN BECAUSE ALL OF THEM HAVE ALSO ATTACHMENT AND AFFECTION WITH YOU." Never allow negativity to accompany impulsiveness and overcome that. This activates automatically once negativity is made to burst, with that the positivity emerges. Then, there is The Living God on Earth. Deep faith and belief works wonders in such situations.

Swami Vivekananda on suicide:

"THE FIRST THING IS NOT TO HATE OURSELVES."

................You will generally hear that this Vedanta, this philosophy and other Eastern systems, look only to something beyond, letting go the enjoyments and struggle of this life. This idea is entirely wrong. It is only ignorant people, who do not know anything of Eastern thought, and never had brain enough to understand anything of its real teaching, that tell you so. On the contrary, we read in our scriptures that our philosophers do not want to go to other worlds, but depreciate them as places where people weep and laugh for a little while only and then die. As long as we are weak we shall have to go through these experiences; but whatever is true, is here, and that is the human soul. And this also is insisted upon, that by committing suicide, we cannot escape the inevitable; we cannot evade it. But the right path is hard to find. The Hindu is just as practical as the Western, only we differ in our views of life.................."

There is also another way, simple, to conquer the negativity and depression. Mind is like a floating boat in the water regardless which direction it takes and which shore of the sea it reaches. If one happens to be in that boat, one's fear is one would sink, that is giving up the hope. It is not so. Boat has to reach shore that is the functional character of sea, the only thing one does not know is which shore it would reach. Since one may not be knowing the navigating the boat, that makes one further fearsome which is not called for because the boat is bound to reach some shore and, that is assured by the sea.

"For, the ocean is big and my boat is small. Find the courage: Alanis Morissette". "Boat is nothing without water and man without his dreams! Mehmet Murat ildan." Most of us believe and act according to what comes from one's mind. As noted, mind doesn't have any form. Its form is ego embedded in the humans. Mind is also not independent. It draws its behavioural features or acts from the conscious, to perform. Mind always lives in wandering and wavering mood. Entire exercise is to crystallize and centralize that mood. One may ask how it could be humanly possible. It would be possible and that possibility has been proved by the great spiritual leaders and saints in our country and in the world. I know that we are not those great spiritual leaders or saints. Being ordinary human beings engaged in life activities – actions at work place and home- to earn and survive oneself. For such humans also, it is possible. How?

Give ten minutes every day, to start with, at whatever time and wherever one is and try to find that golden time from out of one's busiest life. Gradually try to increase the duration up to twenty minutes week after week. It all depends on each individual's constraints and choice. This is so because, we don't believe that the success or failure of the busiest life itself is dependent on how much calm and quiet one is – that is something that guides and leads one to self-satisfaction and, when one is self-satisfied, he or she acquires the capacity and capabilities to convince and satisfy others for whom the work or activity is undertaken. It subsumes the confidence and self-conviction and occupies a position that can answer anything and everything asked. This generates in oneself satisfaction and contentment and a feeling that one has done his or her best for achieving the success equivalent to responsibility vested and the remuneration received.

Next is what to do during those ten or twenty minutes. “Dhayna”. “Dhayna means "contemplation, reflection". It also refers to "imaginative vision". Dhayna is abstract meditation and not the meditation as ordinarily understood. Abstract meditation, according to “Abs-Tract Organization - Medium” means “to retreat, to introspect, to practice solitude and equanimity, in order to find meditation in its simplest and purist form.” When one meditates, he or she is abstracting the self. The stage after that meditation itself is Dhayna. But, both of them are concentration only.

The difference is – Meditation is an Objective Concentration; Dhayna means Subjective Concentration.” If one has to practice meditation, one has to concentrate on her or him. First, one must feel freely ready or available to do during that duration of time. Sit at home or anywhere else where one enjoys freedom to do – one can sit on a mat, a chair, a sofa, on bed at place earmarked for daily prayers or any other place with folded legs and hands. When one wants to sit on the floor, one should sit on a mat. There has to be disconnection between earth and Dhayna otherwise, the earth draws the energy that is being built through Dhayna. There need not be any photo of God or candle or idol or anything of that kind. Just sit with eyes closed.

Allow the mind to wander wherever it wants. Never try to stop it. Just watch within. Mind may take one to Himalayas, Heaven, loved ones, and relationships, to America, to London, to Antarctica and so on. Let it move around the world. Never be attentive to that. Sit in a straight position with eyes closed. If one tries to stop movement of the mind, one gets touched to earthly happenings or the object. That is what is intended to be avoided when one sits with closed eyes. During Dhayna, one can develop an 'imaginative vision" of any kind one finds appealing to self. Suggested time, as far as possible, could be any time between 7 pm and 9 pm before dinner. Go on practicing it daily. After about three months or so, if one had been sincerely and faithfully practicing, one feels a chilling effect in the body. Once that chilling effect happens in the body that signals reverting of the mind from wandering, gradually and settling or say, process of quietening the mind begins. Quietening the mind is the emergence of signs of concentration in mind. The concentration enhances gradually with the intensity of one's sincerity and faith while practising. This exercise should form integral part of life like food and sleep. Never give it up. Feel what wonders the concentration bestows upon the doer. One may be doing gym daily at home or outside but that exercise helps one to build physical strength while Dhayna builds spiritual strength.

Spiritual strength is stronger than physical strength; physical strength is scared of injury while Dhayna is mainly concerned with minimize the mental injury caused by physical injury. All great saints and sages and those learned and realized strive and practice for attaining Quietitude. They do that in their own way. A Karmic can also attain Quietitude practising the method mentioned. Beginning of concentration in one's mind gives impetus to achieve excellence in whatever one wants to do living in busy life. Few Quotes with sources: "I am not what happened to me. I am what I chose to become." (Carl Jung), "Love people for who they are and not for who you want them to be" (Alex

Elle) and "The serenity implied by Quietitude does not in any way exclude the external activities and involvement. In fact the attainment of this enlightened subjective depth and fullness empowers one to pursue activities to a far greater magnitude while remaining anchored to the action less subject within what more? It has its unique sublimating influence on everything around be it a place, a person or an event." (Swami Bhoomananda Tirtha).

Quietitude – means

calm, calmness, hush, peace, peacefulness, placidity, quiet, quietness, repose, restfulness, sereneness, serenity, still, stillness, tranquillity. Once Quietitude is settled, the mind remains under self-control. Quietitude opens up through regular practice invincible link between the mind and the Soul (Atman). How the doer would know it? Doer while practising with faith and humbleness daily, finds vibrations in the body like the folded hands moving upward of their own towards the forehead or the legs showing the signs of lifting up, also signs of expansion of the body, not in physical form but in spiritual form. On feeling this kind of experience or the signals, one should start shifting focus slowly towards the Soul (Atman) that resides deep in the Heart, invisible to human eyes even when the Heart is opened for surgery. Soul or Atman means 'eternal self'. The Atman refers to the real self beyond ego or false self. It is often referred to as 'spirit' or 'soul' and indicates our true self or essence which underlies our existence. The continuous practice takes self to Heightened Consciousness, that is, heightened consciousness used as a term for a permanent state of exalted spiritual awareness with a largely extinguished ego is something else again. That

Heightened Conscious enlightens and enlarges one's knowledge and helps in every aspect of life.

Quietitude is not to be misunderstood as practicing quietness all through the day whether one is walking, standing, talking, crossing, working, in meetings, presentation and so on. These are part of routine life. One has to do what is expected of from one's duty in whatever capacity according to the official code and prevailing circumstances. Duty is also God. Quietitude resides within even while doing the duties and various kinds of necessities in the working place. Those who are able to establish Quietitude within, it is always heard within and not outside. That is, whatever may be the duty or activity one is performing is able to draw the concentration and orderliness of doing for doing so and such concentration and orderliness makes one to achieve excellence and appreciation. Because, one is to understand that if he or she were to be in a state of mind not accomplished with Quietitude, the behavioural pattern of the state of mind is unpredictable, there being no centric force to control it and that leads, many times, to fear, loss of confidence, nervousness, memory loss, a psychological signal that one has not been able to do what was expected of him or her. Quietitude acts as strength to intellectual capacity and physical efforts.

Above approach through the spiritual force of concentration gathered and fixed in the mind binds the mind to always look towards positivity. Thus, the negativity gets itself dissolved in the mind. Dhayna further adds strength to maintain and practice the positivity in life. Life in such a state of mind is hardly concerned with the abstracts and diversions and enables the doer to place the positive energy and the concentrated effort in workplace or home or elsewhere to achieve excellence and outstanding results and achievements in life. Take it to heart and carry forward practice to touch the heart of those who are undergoing negativity and depression. They will be greatly obliged for having brought them back to their normal life and to look for a better and brighter future. They feel there is Living God on Earth. Psychological and other kinds of treatments help ease the intensity of the negativity or depression. Spiritual practice such as Dhayna that has been dealt in the earlier part succeeds in overthrowing the negativity including depression and establishing positivity. Spiritual practice is self-generated through spiritual means and efforts while other kinds of treatments are mechanically tested.

Swami Vivekananda said "The easiest way to get hold of the mind is to sit quiet and let it drift where it will for a while. Hold fast to the idea, "I am the witness watching my mind drifting. The mind is not I." Then see it think as if it were a thing entirely apart from yourself. Identify yourself with God, never with matter or with the mind. Picture the mind as a calm lake stretched before you and the thoughts that come and go as bubbles rising and breaking on its surface. Make no effort to control the thoughts, but watch them and follow them in imagination as they float away. This will gradually lessen the circles. For the mind ranges over wide circles of thought and those circles widen out into ever increasing circles, as in a pond when we throw a stone into it. We want to reverse the process and starting with a huge circle make it narrower until at last

we can fix the mind on one point and make it stay there. Hold to the idea, "I am not the mind, I see that I am thinking, I am watching my mind act', and each day the identification of yourself with thought and feeling will grow less, until at last you can entirely separate yourself from the mind and actually know it to be apart from yourself. When this is done, the mind is your servant to control as you will. The first stage of being a yogi is to go beyond the senses. When the mind is conquered, he has reached the highest stage."

In a human or other conscious being, the element, part, substance, or process that reasons, thinks, feels, wills, perceives, judges, etc.: the processes of the human mind. ... Reason, sanity, or sound mental condition: to lose one's mind, a way of thinking and feeling; disposition; temper: a liberal mind. Ego is the part of the mind that mediates between the conscious and the unconscious and is responsible for reality testing and a sense of personal identity. It represents the person, the mind in itself not having any form, acts both in positive and negative ways depending upon the leads it gets from the intellect (conscious). Intellect becomes wisdom when it securely lodges in the mind, according to Dr. S. Radhakrishnan, noted before. If that does not happen, it thinks independent of Soul or the Self thus breaking its connect with that Source of Life, rather it becomes indifferent to that Source, the Conscience that is capable of discriminating what is good and what is bad of what a person intends to do or not to do. Being forced by the leads of the conscious, the mind conveys to the senses that triggers into ultimate commissioning of an act. An act whether it is good or bad is understandable by a person only when he or she is able to establish and maintain a discernable connection between himself or herself with the spiritual route to feel the pulse of the God manifested in Soul or Self which further links to Conscience that cautions the person what he or she intends to do is good or bad. What ultimately a human does or acts, he alone become answerable to that and also undergo the painful process in life. That linkage is the ever shining expression of spirituality honestly and sincerely understood and followed. When there is a conflict between the Conscience and Conscious, Conscience must prevail. This is Living God.

This is the sum and substance of the **'LIFE IS TO LIVE TOGETHER'** according to the GOLDEN guiding lines that have been given in the foregoing part of this book.

Ways to Show Love in Times of Struggle

1. **Respect one another**: Respect everyone for who they are and what they are going through. Respect can be shown in many ways, from simply listening to someone to offering helpful advice.
2. **Lend a helping hand**: Take the initiative to help out when someone is struggling. Whether it's with a project, an emotional situation, or a physical task, show them you care by helping out.
3. **Offer kind words**: Show your support and understanding with encouraging words and phrases. Even a simple "I'm here for you" can go a long way in showing someone that you care.
4. **Give a hug**: Physical touch can be incredibly powerful when it comes to providing comfort and solace. Hugging someone during a difficult time

shows that you are there for them and that you care deeply.

5. Send a thoughtful note: Writing a heartfelt letter or card can be a meaningful way to show love during hard times. The act of taking the time to put pen to paper speaks volumes about how much you care for the other person.

The Benefits of Togetherness

1. **Support**: When we come together as one, we are able to provide each other with support and comfort in times of struggle. It is reassuring to know that you have someone you can rely on and count on to lift your spirits up when things get tough.
2. **Growth**: Working together helps us to achieve our goals more effectively and efficiently. Through collaboration, we are able to brainstorm ideas, learn from each other's mistakes, and grow our skills and knowledge together.
3. **Happiness**: Togetherness brings a feeling of happiness and contentment. It is easier to appreciate the small victories when we are surrounded by friends and family who understand what we are going through and can celebrate with us.
4. **Strength**: Togetherness gives us strength in numbers. We are no longer alone in our endeavours but rather surrounded by an entire group who can help us stay focused and motivated to reach our goals.
5. **Unity:** Lastly but most importantly, togetherness gives us a sense of unity and belonging. Knowing that we are all going through the same struggles allows us to form a bond that cannot be broken."

[Source: The Power of Togetherness: Why We All Need Each Other to Succeed - Bryce P. Bottom of Form - Cancún, uintana Roo, Mexico – Published 08 March, 2023 – LinkedIn]

"WE CAN ALL GET MORE TOGETHER THAN WE CAN APART. AND THIS IS THE WAY WE GAIN POWER. POWER IS THE ABILITY TO ACHIEVE PURPOSE, POWER IS THE ABILITY TO EFFECT CHANGE, AND WE NEED POWER." - — MARTIN LUTHER KING JR., THE AUTOBIOGRAPHY OF MARTIN LUTHER KING, JR.

"You may be part of a blended family, an adoptive family, or any variation of other family structures. Regardless of how you define family, your feeling of love and togetherness is forever at the core of the unit.

➢ Our shared love and devotion to each other is what makes us a family.

➢ Sharing bloodlines doesn't bond families together, love does.

➢ Choosing to be a family together takes far more strength and love than genetics.

➢ The day we decided to connect our lives together forever, was the day we became family.

➢ I choose you as my family, every minute, every hour and every day, forever.

➢ We don't share DNA, we share FNA: Family Never Abandons.

➢ Together we make a perfect family puzzle.

"SHARING BLOODINESS DOESN'T BOND FAMILIES TOGETHER, LOVE DOES" – [Source: 'Love to Know' Website Page]

"LIVING TOGETHER IS AN ART. IT'S A PATIENT ART, IT'S A BEAUTIFUL ART, IT'S FASCINATING." — POPE FRANCIS

You were standing at a particular place free of any hurricane or whirlwind and when you changed the place of your standing without any reasoning, you found frequent hurricane or whirlwind when it struck your mind that former place is much safer than the latter. Then you landed in two minds and found yourself unable to stick to your mind when you desired to consult someone else, he or she who misguided you more than guiding you. This is based on what we are witnessing around the world.

A SMILING LIE IS A WHIRLWIND, EASY TO ENTER, BUT HARD TO ESCAPE.- DEJAN STOJANOVIC

"WHEN YOU'RE IN LOVE, LOVE MAKES YOU DO CRAZY THINGS, AND CAN TAKE YOU DOWN A WHIRLWIND OF A ROAD". KEVIN HART

Self-belief and understanding is the core of intelligence and permanency of comfort. Let us learn to live together as we consider more beneficial to humans than quarrelsome and constant bickering that make our mind a floating fool not realizing that we are heading towards that end by living apart. Seeking advice and guidance is good depending upon how much one is inclined to do so. Such practice should not be made a daily chorus in one's life. One who is rendering advice and guidance is also born on Mother Earth and learnt certain art. This is a learnt but not natural art. Natural art is blessed. by Mother Earth or the God to one seeking sincerely and honestly for benefit of others than for himself or herself. That is what we can learn from the Holy Scriptures of the Great Saints and Sages. They were true to themselves and believed always about the good of others.

As noted at the beginning of this book, human life is rarest of the rare that gives birth on Mother Earth according to the sayings of the Great Saints and Sages. The Hindu Newspaper states in an Article 'Invaluable human birth

November 04, 2013', among others that "For a Jivatma, to be born as a human among the innumerable species of life, is itself a unique blessing in the arduous journey through countless births. Human birth provides the exclusive opportunity to pursue the Purusharthas — dharma (righteousness), wealth (artha), desire (kama) and salvation (moksha). Even in the brief life span, there is the inbuilt chance to gain access to knowledge of God, experience His infinite greatness, and seek salvation, observed Swami Bhoomananda Tirtha during a lecture on Vedanta in life. In this context, he referred to Krishna's expositions to Arjuna in the Bhagavad Gita, emphasising the need for focused perception to augment the rare human faculties of mind, speech and intellect."

"The human body resonates at the same frequency as Mother Earth. So instead of only focusing on trying to save the earth, which operates in congruence to our vibrations, I think it is more important to be one with each other. If you really want to remedy the earth, we have to mend mankind. And to unite mankind, we heal the Earth. That is the only way. Mother Earth will exist

with or without us. Yet if she is sick, it is because mankind is sick and separated. And if our vibrations are bad, she reacts to it, as do all living creatures." - — Suzy Kassem, Rise Up and Salute the Sun: The Writings of Suzy Kassem

Weighing scales are tools used to measure weight or compute mass. The first mass-measuring device was the balance, commonly referred to as a balance scale or beam balance. The beam and a weighing pan are attached to a horizontal lever that pivots and has equal-length arms in the typical configuration. Live like a weighing scale.

Meta-analyses of love scales: Do various love scales measure the same psychological constructs? - WILEY Meta-analyses of love scales: - Masahiro Masuda -First published: 03 February 2003 [Excerpts]

"........**Abstract**: Two statistical meta-analyses synthesized 33 empirical studies which investigated the correlation between relationship satisfaction and two types of love: Erotic Love and Companionate Love, measured by various love scales based on four major theories by Rubin, Lee, Hatfield and Sternberg. The results drawn by the Hunter-Schmidt method showed that satisfaction was highly correlated with Erotic Love, but that its correlation with Companionate Love was unclear due to heterogeneity in the total sample of the all Companionate Love studies. A moderator analysis indicated a potential moderator, that is, theoretical differences between Lee's Color Theory of Love and the other three theories. The result suggested that a Companionate Love named "Storge" in the Color Theory should not be mixed up with other friendship-style loves defined by other theories as the Storge subscale would measure a different psychological construct..................

Discussion

The results show an intriguing contrast between E-Love and C-Love. Whereas E-Love in all theories seemed to measure the same psychological constructs, the meta-analysis of C-Love seemed to have attempted to blend different qualities; apparently, Color Theory Scales and Other Theories Scales seem to measure different psychological constructs rather than the same characteristics of "friendship-like" love.

Why are these two friendship-like loves so different? I assume that this difference originates in theoretical definitions between Storge and other C-Loves. As noted earlier, Lee's (1973) Color Theory identifies six prototypes of love, while Sternberg (1986) posits summative models based on three constituents of love; therefore, each prototype is supposed to be significantly distinguished from the other five. Furthermore, Lee's Color Theory demarcates six prototypes whereas Hatfield and Walster (1978) attempted to explain the nature of love by the dichotomy between Passionate Love and Companionate Love; therefore, it is probable that Lee's Storge represents a narrower sense of C-Love than Rubin's (1970) love, Hatfield's Companionate Love, or Sternberg's Intimacy. The latter three C-Loves do not deny the passion in romantic feelings as Storge does; these C-Love scales simply do not ask questions about psychological arousal and physical attraction.

Indeed, the current study has a limitation that the meta-analyses synthesized only research articles available in the US, and only those written in English. This meta-analysis should be revised by the inclusion of more data published in Japanese and other non-English languages. Despite its limitation, however, this meta-analytic study presents thought-provoking findings which contribute to the integration of love theories and research findings based on these theories. This meta-analysis indicates potential differences in conceptualization of both E-Love and C-Love among love scales by showing statistical evidence, reminding researchers of how each scale has been constructed. This finding will prevent researchers from mixing up different characteristics of love and also motivate them to posit new love theories for the construction of more universal love scales"

Sage Journals - Family Demography in India: Emerging Patterns and Its Challenges-Swastika Chakravorty https://orcid.org/0000-0003-3681- 50 swa.cha1992@gmail.com, Srinivas Goli https://orcid. org/0000-0002-8481-484X, and K. S. James View all authors and affiliations - https://doi.org/10.1177/ 21582440211008178 [Excerpts]:

"**...............Conclusion and Way Forward**

Demographic studies of the family have not progressed very far conceptually especially visualizing families in different stages of demographic transition in multiple cultural contexts. Despite great efforts by researchers to study family as a unit of analysis, it has been restricted to particular aspects of family life, unable to provide a comprehensive view of the family as a dynamic system related to changes taking place in developing societies such as India. Research has yet to investigate the interrelationships of the family as an operational unit with various other structures of the society and the reciprocal effect of one or other and their interactive effects on individuals. Moreover, in a stable society, roles within families are clearly and consensually defined and understood. During the period of transition, such as in India, these expectations are upset and uncertainties emerge regarding individual responses to these changes. Social, demographic and economic changes are highly skewed processes. Therefore, these processes do not affect each strata of the population evenly. The lag between onset of transitional processes and the stabilization of social, economic, and demographic structures across the population sub-groups is characterized by pre-transition heterogeneity often concealed as conflict and disorganization until the homogeneous progressive phase of transition begins and statuses are redefined according to the new conditions.

Until now, the social institutions and practices in India have been relatively stable but changes are predicted to occur in the next two-three decades. It is imperative to study these changes and their bi-directional relationships with family demography and related behaviors. The main impediment to the study of family demography and related research in India is first the lack of a comprehensive conceptual framework and second lack of reliable data. Understandably, family demography is currently in its nascent stages as a branch of demography and population studies. Fundamental intricacy inherent in demographic conceptualization and differentiation in functions of households and families has rendered this scientifically important area of study rather muted. Western countries such as U.S. and European nations have multiple sources of data such as American Community Survey, Current Population Survey, Organisation for Economic Co-operation and Development (OECD) Family Database, Fertility & Family survey, and so on, which provide information on a wide range of issues pertaining to family demography and related domains at sub-national level. Even developing countries like Nepal, Bangladesh, China have family panel surveys focused on intergenerational exchanges and life-course perspectives at sub-national levels. The dearth of available information on family demography in India and in its states, limits the researchers investigating contemporary and emerging issues such as marital happiness, same-sex marriages their sexual behaviors, quality of marriages, complex families, fatherhood in complex families, family disruptions and its long-term effect on child's economic outcome and multi-dimensional deprivation, and so on."

I have given before ample supporting or opposing views in the Articles also stated before. These are Articles authored by learned Writers based on their own perception or possibly, the experience they have undergone or witnessed in their lives. The readers of this book who are in the midst of such circumstances or situations may or may not be able to agree or cope up with what those Articles have tried to impress upon because reality one is undergoing may differ with one written in the Articles. Yet, it is worth heeding to what is contributed in the Articles to the extent as possible which would hopefully narrow down the psychological distances among the married couple on the verge of breaking down and more, importantly, on the missing parent of a child or growing children.

In the scale of equalization, the married couples becoming more anxious towards breaking, they seem to forget to add to the scale the weight of their child or growing children. If such couple is placing greater weightage on their distancing difference of whatever nature and are endangering the future their child or children back of them. Those married couple who are unfortunately not blessed with a child or children may not be impacted so much about what I submitted before but the fact cannot ignored that such couples are continuing life couples and, most of them, seek for various ways outs including in particular the medical advice in order to be blessed with a child. See the contrast in this aspect. Those who have child or children who need to give highest weightage on the child or children at the time they are thinking of separation, those are denied of the child by the Nature are restlessly seeking to secure a child including, in some case, adoption of a child. The scale of weightage in such cases is much weightier for the couple having child or children while those unfortunate couple not having a child desire to add weightage to the scale in order to balance it since the scale, in such cases, remains blank on the one side.

Most valuable asset to the married couple is birth of a child or children in lifetime than what each is comparing one's weight with the other. Once marriage is consummated between the two persons [wife and husband], it is to be presumed that the marriage has been made in the heaven which fact or presumption should be accepted sincerely and honestly between each other that opens up the doors to welcome the newly born child. Those couple who under estimate the essence and importance of a child for the continuance of lineage for reason of their own squabbling or conflict or confrontation in their relationship, such couple have not understood the meaning of jewels. Whichever woman may be, she wants to wear jewels in one form or the other, that is a natural desire. Those who are blessed with child or children who is or are jewels of the family, more decorating the status of the couple, than the physical decoration for; physical decoration is occasional and artificial while natural decoration that is embedded in a child is more valuable and worthy of according increasing protection and pleasure.

Why I have touched so much about a child or children? Every question brings a brightening answer whether in a class or in a family. Such God given sentiment does not occur to the married couple who are on the way of breaking, having a child or children. Their fate is left to the Court of Law to adjudicate when divorce takes place whether the child or children will be more protective with the mother or the father. This is the critical Question every married couple should seek for a valid and practical answer before entertaining any idea of breaking each other. A wooden structure is alterable but a natural structure once altered cannot be recreated and, if recreated, that will be through repairs. Let us not grow poison at home planted by someone else.

The efforts made in this book are intended to the citizens of the country and the married couples. I sincerely and hopefully believe the readers would be kind enough to dwell upon realism than irreality on making the Life as a

Living Together aspiration. The Live-in-Partner concept is like green leaves on the top of the tree not knowing whether or not either of the partner has the inclinatory strength to sustain his or her relationship when he or she sees the drying up the leaves on the top of the tree. The tree is bound to grow again green leaves, the natural process of the Nature but whether or not that happens in Live-in-Partner life not being natural process of the Nature. The process that is not as per the natural process is prone to dangers to life of one or the other partner as we are witnessing today how such relationship is working in real life. When criminal intent manifests in such relationship, the relationship ends up in a more tragical manner unbearable to even read or learn in the media leave alone the most tragical consequences stand outside the door.

Let us also appreciate and understand that Life is made to Live Togtether as God has bestowed upon humans and, that way, humans should be grateful to God. Anyone is free to deviate from this bestowedness but one should know what deviation brings at the end of the day of the Life.

Every second has goodness, every minute has goodness, every hour has goodness and every day has goodness if one incorporates the sense of goodness in one's heart. What do we mean by goodness anyway? It is defined, in part, as...

1. Moral excellence; virtue.
2. Kindly feeling; kindness; generosity.
3. Excellence of quality.

If we want to improve our increasingly polarized, broken, and too often uncivil and corrupt world then we should place more emphasis on goodness as an important virtue to nurture in ourselves and in others as well. And in the spirit of the groundbreaking research of psychologist Albert Bandura on observational learning, we should attend to goodness behavior, model it, repeat it, and help people to be motivated to engage in it as well. We want to create a culture where goodness is highlighted, reinforced, and encouraged in all aspects of life and for everyone. [Source: Goodness: An Often Underrated but Much Needed Virtue by Thomas G. Plante – September 1, 2016 – Posted on Psychology Today]

"DO YOUR LITTLE BIT OF GOOD WHERE YOU ARE; IT'S THOSE LITTLE BITS OF GOOD PUT TOGETHER THAT OVERWHELM THE WORLD."

— DESMOND TUTU

ABOUT THE AUTHOR

[Note: The recounting given hereunder is long due to misfortune and trauma that happened in my life.]

Graduate in Commerce 1961. Completed short Vigilance Course organized by the Institute of Secretariat Training & Management and in Parliamentary Procedures and Practices organized by the Bureau of Parliamentary Studies & Training, Ten days on job training in World Bank (1990), Washington. I was a Team Member of the World Bank and ADB Teams for Project Appraisal and Special Studies. A Member of the Loan Negotiation Team of the Government of India for ADB Loan for financing power projects in the county.

I served Rural Electrification Corporation Limited {REC} for 18 years and Power Finance Corporation Limited {PFC} for 12 years, overall 30 years.

While I was working in Rural Electrification Corporation Limited (REC) as Deputy Secretary, my services were sought by the erstwhile Ministry of Energy [now Ministry of Power] for drafting of Memorandum of Association [MOA] and Articles of Association [AOA'], other related documents and for registration/incorporation of PFC. PFC was incorporated on 16 July, 1986 under the Companies Act, 1956 after due approvals and as per the procedure prescribed under Company Law. My services were again sought by the same Ministry on immediate basis in the first week of September, 1987 for raising Rs. 100 Cr. from the financial market [Public Issue] including its utilization for critical power projects selected by the Planning Commission by end of March, 1988 as per the mandate stated to have been given to the Ministry by the MOF/PMO. I joined PFC on 17th September, 1987 on deputation as Senior Manager [Bonds] for a period of one year. Besides registration, I functionalized and operationalized the PFC.

CMD was yet to be appointed. I was reporting to Joint Secretary (F) in the Ministry. CMD assumed office on 14th January, 1988.

The entire amount was mobilized and utilized for the projects as mandated by the end of March, 1988 after due approvals and loan documentation by the Board of Directors [BOD] of PFC. PFC awarded to me honorarium and commendation letter. As per the desire of CMD, I absorbed in the services of PFC after one year in the same post as Employee Number One (001) of PFC. I was promoted from that post to the post of Deputy General Manager [Finance & Financial Operations] in 1989 in PFC..

As my moral duty, I wish to state that at the fag end of my services in PFC, I was implicated in a politically motivated criminal case when the security scam broke out in 1992, in connection with investment transactions of around Rs. 419 Cr. made with a UCO Bank, Hamam Street Branch, Mumbai, even though the fact being that the investment transactions related to 1988-90 and had no relationship with security scam for which the government established a Special Court under the Special Court [Trial of Offences

Relating to Transactions in Securities] Act, 1992 in Mumbai.

The entire invested amount alongwith the interest due and payable thereon was received back by PFC on due dates. The need for investment with the above Bank arose as the New Delhi Local Branch of the said Bank to whom PFC approached for empanelment of its name for absorption of short term surplus funds for investment in Government Securities/Public Sector Bonds. Such letters were addressed by the then CMD to the Chief Executives of the SBI, its subsidiaries and Nationalized Banks in April, every year. The said Branch advised PFC that the investments in securities are dealt by its Branch at the Hamam Street Branch, Mumbai, which was said to be solely dealing in securities transactions through its Official Brokers under the instructions of its Head Office.

PFC did not file any complaint against me with the CBI. CBI registered the case suomoto.

The then CMD appeared before the Joint Parliamentary Committee (JPC) in connection with investment of Rs. 300 Cr in March, 1992 made by him, the period covered under Securities Scam by obtaining offer directly from Harshad Mehta's firm which was the officially appointed broker firm of the UCO Bank, Hamam Street Branch, Mumbai. The amount was invested by him in equal amount with UCO Bank, Hamam Street Branch through the said Broker's firm and the Citi Bank, New Delhi. The then CMD admitted before JPC having invested the above amount and through said banks and broker.

Due to tremendous political pressure brought upon due to JPC findings, soon thereafter, I was placed under suspension in November 1992. On appeal in the Hon'ble High Court of Delhi and the Orders passed by the Hon'ble High Court, the suspension order was revoked in May; 1996. I remained under suspension for four and a half years.

The then CMD who was examined by JPC in connection with the investment of Rs. 300 Cr. Stated before, accorded sanction for prosecution against me. The Charge Sheet was filed in 1994 and the Approver's Statement was filed in 1996.The charge sheet and Approver's Statement do not mention a word about any allegation against me of corruption or recovery from me or any of my relatives or of any financial loss to PFC. The Search Report given to me by the CBI was submitted to the said CMD the same day for his kind information.

The Statutory Auditor's Report incorporated in the Annual Report of PFC for 1992-93 {P 39, Para 1. Page 40 Para 11.6 and Page 41 Para 4, 5, 9 Point 26.1} regarding investment of Rs. 300 Cr. stated before supports the mala-fide intention of the then CMD in sanction of prosecution against me. PFC suffered financial loss of Rs.15 Cr under the above investment. The amount is stated to have been written off in the books of accounts. There was no criminal or departmental action against those who caused financial loss of Rs. 15 cr. including the said CMD. This was a blatant discrimination on the part of CBI to have charge sheeted me despite no financial loss having caused by me to PFC.

So long as I was entrusted investment department, PFC did all its investment of short term surplus funds through the SBI and its subsidiaries, Nationalized Commercial Banks and their subsidiaries. PFC did not deal investment transactions with any Broker's firm as a matter of policy although its Articles permitted dealing with brokers.

On the mandate of the Nationalized Bank at Mumbai with whom the investment transactions were done, PFC obtained quotes from the Representative of their Official Broker's firm in New Delhi and all the investments, were based on merits of rate and absorbing capacity, duly approved by the then CMD were made in the name of UCO Bank, Hamam Street, Mumbai.

All the investment transactions with the aforesaid Bank were made by RBI Cheques (Banker's Cheques) crossed A/c Payee initially through the New Delhi Main Branch and later, as mandated by the UCO Bank Branch at Hamam Street, Mumbai, the investments were routed through a designated foreign Bank (ANZ Grindlays Bank, Parliament Street, New Delhi) which had said to have the online money transfer through SWIFT transfer facility [Society for Worldwide Interbank Financial Telecommunication] since investment amount was to be transferred on the same day as the interest thereon was to start from the date of the cheque.

PFC had given specific written mandate in the form of letters along with the Banker's Cheque crossed A/c Payee to the said foreign Bank with copy to the Hamam Street Brach of UCO Bank at Mumbai for transfer of money to the invested Bank at Mumbai. The designated foreign bank for transfer, as per the Charge Sheet, credited the proceeds of the banker's cheque to the account of the Broker's firm. It is also stated in the Charge Sheet that the forwarding letters and the banker's cheques were handed over by the concerned Officers in PFC to the local representative of the Harshad Mehta's firm, the Official Broker of UCO Bank, Hamam Street, Mumbai. This was being done by the PFC officials as per the mandate and authorization given in writing by the UCO Bank, Hamam Street at Mumbai to PFC. PFC had also received such mandates from five to six other banks and Crossed RBI Cheques handed over to their Agents under the letter of authorization. The investments made with these banks were properly invested and invested amounts along interest payable were received back by PFC on due dates from all of them. There was no default whatsoever as far as done by the investment department under me.

I was not aware of crediting the banker's cheque proceeds to the account of said Broker's firm by the said foreign bank since all the monies invested together with interest due and payable were received back by PFC on due dates with no loss of funds, thus leaving no scope for suspicion on misuse inasmuch as also, the RBI Crossed cheques were to be deposited in the A/c of PFC maintained with RBI. The Charge Sheet states the Approver had replaced the letter given by PFC enclosing the cheques by the letter of Harshad Mehta firm as per the instructions of Harshad Mehta, the fact of which was not known to PFC which presumed the proceedings of cheques were transferred to UCO Bank, Hamam Street Branch through its designated ANZ Grindlays Bank, New Delhi since Bank Receipts [BR] for the invested funds duly signed by the authorized signatories of the said Bank were furnished to PFC with particulars of securities in which funds were invested and the invested funds along with interest payable thereon were received back by PFC on the due dates and the BR was duly discharged by PFC officials and returned to the said Bank. All these documents form part of the Documents attached by the CBI to the Charge Sheet.

The said CMD ordered special audit of the investment transactions of the value stated before. The special audit report contains the complete procedure followed by the investment department with no adverse comments or qualifications, thus authenticated the investment procedure followed with the approval of the then CMD. The special audit report also specifically confirmed in Part III to the specific queries of CMD to the effect there were no deviations in the investment procedure followed with the said UCO Bank, Hamam Street Branch and the transactions had the approval of the competent authority i.e. the then CMD.

This report was considered by the Central Vigilance Commission (CVC) which requested the Ministry of Energy to forward it to the Director of CBI for taking into consideration while investigating the case. This was accordingly done by the Ministry of Energy (now Power). CBI, except attaching a copy of the same with Charge Sheet as part of the documents (D23), did not mention a single word about the same in the Charge Sheet, thus had not taken the report into consideration during the investigation. The report would have bared the allegations made in the Charge Sheet had CBI taken same into consideration during investigation and had dealt it also in the Charge Sheet. This was biased and prejudicial on the part of the CBI.

I was under depression for about six months after the suspension. I made written submissions to the CMD, PFC, then Secretary in the Ministry and the Hon'ble Minister of Energy but there was no response from any one. My wife developed hypertension in 1993 which could not be controlled despite best medical treatment. She suffered brain stroke 12th May, 2005 midnight, admitted to the hospital, remained in coma for 28 days. On regaining on the 29th day, the Doctors found her having completely paralyzed right side and loss of speech. She remained bed ridden for eight years and passed away on 7th Dec 2013.

The case though registered under the PCA associated with the provisions of IPC was transferred to THE SPECIAL COURT AT BOMBAY Constituted under the Special Court [Trial of Offences Relating to Transactions in Securities] Act, 1992 in Mumbai on the petitions filed by some of the accused persons residing in Mumbai sometime in 2017. On appeal by CBI in Hon'ble Court of Delhi, in 2017, the transfer of case was stayed. Final Order is still awaited. The regular trial is yet to begin. The case has thus been pending for the last more than 30 years.

I was due for retirement on 31st December, 1996; my service was extended up to 31st July, 1997, the date on which I retired from the services of PFC. There being no Pension Scheme in PFC at that time, I served as Consultant in Multinational Consultancy Organizations for 18 years post retirement to financially support myself and my family. PFC engaged me as consultant in May, 2006 for assisting PFC on policy, procedural and compliance matters of SPVs set up by PFC [PFC was the Nodal Agency] under Ultra Mega Power Projects, an Initiative launched by the

GOI/MOP in 2005-06, served PFC in that position for two years on contract basis. In June, 2008 joined another multinational subsidiary company (a Subsidiary of German based Parent Company) as Senior Advisor [Finance, Commercial and Regulatory Affairs], Best Professional Employee and Special Contribution Awards were given to me while working in this company.

I am now aged 87 years and, on that ground and there being no allegation of any recovery nor any financial loss to PFC, filed petition for discharge in the Hon'ble High Court of Delhi which, though appreciated the facts, dismissed the petition as not a fit case on the ground that other accused persons had not filed any such petition. Among the accused persons in the case, I was the only person oldest of all others.

Though I have been Employee No. 001 of PFC, I retired in the same post I was holding on the date of my suspension [DGM-Fin] while my most of the juniors retired as Director and CMD. I thus lost my entire professional future career and the consequent financial benefits.

My Advocate whom I engaged for filing the Petition in the Hon'ble High Court of Delhi and his Associate Advocate filed SLP in the Hon'ble Supreme Court against the Order of Hon'ble High Court of Delhi. On the date of hearing, the Associate Advocate [AOR] withdrew the SLP of his own. AOR did not inform me about the withdrawal of SLP. I came to know about the same after about two months when I contacted his junior Advocate. This also entailed additional expenditure on my part which was met by me elder son who was working in a foreign country.

On completion of the contract in 2018 with multinational Consultancy Company, I took up writing of books. The List of Books published by me numbering 17 is appended. .

More than thirty years are over; the trial is yet to begin. The mental and physical pain is curable by the Doctors but there is no Law under which an accused person can approach for relief for the inordinate and continuing delay in a case in which there was no recovery at all, is, according to me, also a kind of cruelty.

I had submitted several emails to CVC, CBI and PFC for expediting the case but no response. This is the case of victimization of an honest officer in government and criminal system. Some victims die during or before the trial while others are livingly dead till the trial is completed or also die before pronounce of judgment.

No one cares a condemned person even condemnation is not proved as yet after thirty one years. That leaves the person to his fate including death without any condemnation.

THOSE WHO GRANT SYMPATHY TO GUILT, GRANT NONE TO INNOCENCE." - — AYN RAND

LIST OF BOOKS PUBLISHED BY PRAHALAD RAO

[The books hereunder mentioned are registered under The Copy Rights Act, 1957 and ISBNs are incorporated therein]

1. A WAKE UP CALL FOR EVERY INDIAN {2019}
2. JAMMU & KASHMIR – THE TRUTH OF THE MATTER – 2019
3. THE LIVING GOD ON EARTH - 2019
4. PRITHVI PER JEEVIT ISHWAR {2020} { THIS BOOK WAS TRANSLATED IN HINDI LANGUAGE ON DEMAND}
5. SOUNDS OF SILENCES IN INDIA'S CONSTITUTION-DANGERS AHEAD – 2020-
6. COVID-19 – NOT A NATURAL CALAMITY – AN ANALYSIS OF ITS ORIGIN AND THE FALLOUT {2021}
7. INDIA'S POLILTICAL BLUNDERS BLEEDING ITS BOUNDARIES 2021.
8. SOCIALIST, SECULAR & RELIGION IN INDIA – THE MISCONCEPTIONS 2021
9. INDIA'S STRESSED ASSETS CONUNDRUM-SUGGESTED WAYOUT – 2021
10. ANYONE WHO CAN TELL WHERE DID COVID-19 COME FROM THAT KILLED MILLIONS

HUMANS IN THE WORLD – IS SILENCE AN ANSWER? {2021}.

11. ABOUT CERTAIN DECISIONS ON TARIFF UNDER ELECTRICITY ACT, 2003 – IN RETROSPECT {2021}
12. INDIAN PARLIAMENT MONSOON SESSION {2021} RUCKUS – TIME TO THINK ABOUT COURSE OF ACTION.
13. INDIA'S FUTURISTIC DEMOCRACY – THREATS OF CONSTITUTIONAL GAPS AND DIGITAL ERA – DECEMBER, 2022.
14. INDIA'S ELECTIOIN FINANCING, FREEBIES AND WELFARE – A FISCAL DISASTEER [2023].
15. WE ARE ONE INDIA ONE PEOPLE – 2023
16. TRUTH ABOUT THE SECURITIES SCAM 1992 [2023]
17. INDIAN DEMOCRACY'S PARADOXES [2024]
18. LIFE IS TO LIVE TOGETHER [THIS BOOK]

[PUBLISHERS: M/S BLUEROSE PRIVATE COMPANY LIMITED]